LAWS AND LEGISLATION

COPYRIGHT RESTORATION AND THE SUPREME COURT'S GOLAN V. HOLDER DECISION

LAWS AND LEGISLATION

Additional books in this series can be found on Nova's website
under the Series tab.

Additional E-books in this series can be found on Nova's website
under the E-book tab.

CONGRESSIONAL POLICIES, PRACTICES AND PROCEDURES

Additional books in this series can be found on Nova's website
under the Series tab.

Additional E-books in this series can be found on Nova's website
under the E-book tab.

LAWS AND LEGISLATION

COPYRIGHT RESTORATION AND THE SUPREME COURT'S GOLAN V. HOLDER DECISION

NICHOLAS A. HERNANDEZ
AND
AMY KING
EDITORS

Nova Science Publishers, Inc.
New York

For permission to use material from this book please contact us:
Telephone 631-231-7269; Fax 631-231-8175
Web Site: http://www.novapublishers.com

Additional color graphics may be available in the e-book version of this book.

LIBRARY OF CONGRESS CATALOGING-IN-PUBLICATION DATA

ISBN: 978-1-62081-174-0

Published by Nova Science Publishers, Inc. † New York

CONTENTS

Preface		**vii**
Chapter 1	Congress's Power to Restore Copyright Protection to Works That Have Entered the Public Domain: *Golan v. Holder* *Brian T. Yeh*	**1**
Chapter 2	Supreme Court of the United States	**15**
Index		**67**

PREFACE

This book examines the Golan v. Holder Supreme Court Case, which discussed whether Congress has the power to grant copyright protection to creative works that have already entered the public domain. A group of orchestra conductors, educators, performers, film archivists, and motion picture distributors, who had relied on the free and unrestricted availability of these artistic works in the public domain for their livelihoods, filed a lawsuit against the federal government challenging the constitutionality of the URAA.

Chapter 1 - On October 5, 2011, the U.S. Supreme Court heared oral argument in *Golan v. Holder,* a case considering whether Congress had the power under the Copyright Clause of the U.S. Constitution to grant copyright protection to creative works that have already entered the public domain. In 1994, Congress enacted the Uruguay Round Agreements Act (URAA) of 1994[1]; Section 514 of the URAA "restored" copyright protection to certain foreign works that had been in the U.S. public domain, in order to bring the United States into compliance with the Berne Convention for the Protection of Literary and Artistic Works of 1886, which the United States had joined in 1989. These foreign works had lost or never obtained copyright protection in the United States because their creators failed to comply with certain mandatory statutory formalities that were required by the federal Copyright Act at that time, such as filing registrations with the U.S. Copyright Office or affixing copyright notice to them (identifying the copyright owner and date of publication).

Chapter 2 - The Berne Convention for the Protection of Literary and Artistic Works (Berne), which took effect in 1886, is the principal accord governing international copyright relations. Berne's 164 member states agree to provide a minimum level of copyright protection and to treat authors from other member countries as well as they treat their own. Of central importance in this case, Article 18 of Berne requires countries to protect the works of other member states unless the works' copyright term has expired in either the country where protection is claimed or the country of origin. A different system of transnational copyright protection long prevailed in this country. Throughout most of the 20th century, the only foreign authors eligible for Copyright Act protection were those whose countries granted reciprocal rights to American authors and whose works were printed in the United States. Despite Article 18, when the United States joined Berne in 1989, it did not protect any foreign works lodged in the U. S. public domain, many of them works never protected here. In 1994, however, the Agreement on Trade-Related Aspects of Intellectual Property Rights mandated implementation of Berne's first 21 articles, on pain of enforcement by the World Trade Organization.

In: Copyright Restoration …
Editors: N. Hernandez, A. King

ISBN: 978-1-62081-174-0

Chapter 1

CONGRESS'S POWER TO RESTORE COPYRIGHT PROTECTION TO WORKS THAT HAVE ENTERED THE PUBLIC DOMAIN: *GOLAN V. HOLDER*[*]

Brian T. Yeh

SUMMARY

Golan v. Holder is a case heard by the U.S. Supreme Court on October 5, 2011. The Court considered whether Congress has the power to grant copyright protection to creative works that have already entered the public domain. At issue in *Golan* is the Uruguay Round Agreements Act (URAA) of 1994 that Congress passed in order to bring the United States into compliance with international agreements on intellectual property (IP). Section 514 of the URAA "restored" copyrights in certain foreign works that were previously in the public domain in the United States. After these works became protected by copyright as a result of URAA, anyone wishing to use them needs to seek prior permission from the copyright holders and also likely pay licensing fees. Although it is difficult to determine the exact number of foreign works that the URAA removed from the public domain, the former Register of Copyrights estimated that it may be in the millions.

---

[*] This is an edited, reformatted and augmented version of Congressional Research Service, Publication No. R41977, dated August 30, 2011.

A group of orchestra conductors, educators, performers, film archivists, and motion picture distributors, who had relied on the free and unrestricted availability of these artistic works in the public domain for their livelihoods, filed a lawsuit against the federal government challenging the constitutionality of the URAA. The U.S. Court of Appeals for the Tenth Circuit determined that § 514 of the URAA was within Congress's power under the Copyright Clause and that it did not violate the free speech and expression rights of the plaintiffs who had enjoyed freely using the foreign works that were in the U.S. public domain before the restoration of their copyright protection.

The Supreme Court's ruling in *Golan v. Holder* is expected to provide definitive answers to the following significant questions in copyright law: whether Congress is prohibited by the Copyright Clause from taking works out of the public domain, and whether § 514 of the URAA violates the First Amendment to the U.S. Constitution.

INTRODUCTION

On October 5, 2011, the U.S. Supreme Court heared oral argument in *Golan v. Holder,* a case considering whether Congress had the power under the Copyright Clause of the U.S. Constitution to grant copyright protection to creative works that have already entered the public domain. In 1994, Congress enacted the Uruguay Round Agreements Act (URAA) of 1994[1]; Section 514 of the URAA "restored" copyright protection to certain foreign works that had been in the U.S. public domain, in order to bring the United States into compliance with the Berne Convention for the Protection of Literary and Artistic Works of 1886, which the United States had joined in 1989. These foreign works had lost or never obtained copyright protection in the United States because their creators failed to comply with certain mandatory statutory formalities that were required by the federal Copyright Act at that time, such as filing registrations with the U.S. Copyright Office or affixing copyright notice to them (identifying the copyright owner and date of publication).

In 2001, a group of artists, performers, businesses, teachers, publishers, archivists, and movie distributors who had depended on artistic works in the public domain for their livelihoods, filed a lawsuit against the federal government challenging the constitutionality of the URAA. They argued that (1) the law's restoration of copyrights in foreign works that had been in the public domain interfered with their First Amendment rights to use, perform, and distribute them, and (2) the law exceeded the Congress's authority under the Copyright Clause. The U.S. Court of Appeals rejected these constitutional arguments in two separate rulings, holding that § 514 of the URAA was a valid exercise of Congress's power[2] and that it did not violate the plaintiffs' free speech rights because the law is a content-neutral regulation of speech that was narrowly tailored to serve a substantial or important governmental interest—securing copyright protection for American works in foreign countries, as many of the United States' trading partners (who were signatories to the Berne Convention) had made clear that they would restore American copyrights that were in their public domain only if the United States restored foreign copyrights.[3]

The U.S. Supreme Court granted the plaintiffs' petition for a writ of certiorari on March 7, 2011, in order to consider the following questions:

1) Does the Copyright Clause of the United States Constitution prohibit Congress from taking works out of the public domain?
2) Does Section 514 of the URAA violate the First Amendment of the United States Constitution?

BACKGROUND

Brief Overview of Copyright Law

The source of federal copyright law originates with the Copyright Clause (also referred to as the Progress Clause) of the U.S. Constitution, which authorizes Congress to "promote the Progress of Science[4] ... by securing for limited Times to Authors ... the exclusive Right to their respective Writings."[5] Therefore, this constitutional provision indicates that the rights conferred by a copyright cannot last forever; rather, a copyright holder may exercise his/her exclusive rights only for "limited Times." At the expiration of that period of time, the copyrighted work becomes part of the public domain, available for anyone to use without payment of royalties or permission. The U.S. Supreme Court has opined that "[t]he primary objective of copyright is not to reward the labor of authors, but 'to promote the Progress of Science and useful Arts.'"[6]

The Copyright Act grants legal protection to the creator or owner of certain original works[7] of creative expression, including books, movies, photography, art, and music.[8] The Copyright Act refers to the creator of such works as an "author"; ownership of a copyright initially vests in the author,[9] but the author may transfer ownership of the copyright to another person or company.[10] Copyright protection does not extend to any underlying abstract idea, procedure, process, system, method of operation, concept, principle, or discovery, but rather it only protects the manner in which those ideas are expressed.[11]

A copyright holder possesses several exclusive legal entitlements under the Copyright Act, including the rights of reproduction, distribution, public performance, and public display of the protected material, that provide the holder with the power to determine whether and under what circumstances the protected work may be used by third parties.[12] If a copyright holder chooses to allow a third party to exercise one of the exclusive rights provided by the copyright, such permission is often granted in the form of a license, which is usually expressed in a written contract. [13] The terms of a licensing agreement may include certain limitations on using the copyrighted work and may require payment of a royalty fee.

The Copyright Act contains several statutory limitations on the copyright monopoly. These include the "first sale doctrine"[14] that limits the copyright owner's exclusive control over distribution of the material objects in which a work is expressed. The "first sale doctrine" permits the owner of a particular copy of a copyrighted work to sell or dispose of that copy without the copyright owner's permission. Other limitations involve allowing certain reproductions by libraries and archives,[15] limited performances and displays for educational purposes or in the course of services at a place of worship,[16] and certain performances for non-profit, charitable causes.[17] The doctrine of "fair use" in copyright law recognizes the right of the public to make reasonable use of copyrighted material, under particular circumstances, without the copyright holder's consent. For example, a teacher may be able to use reasonable excerpts of copyrighted works in preparing a scholarly lecture or commentary, without obtaining permission to do so. The Copyright Act mentions fair use "for purposes such as criticism, comment, news reporting, teaching, scholarship, or research."[18] However, a determination of fair use requires a federal court to engage in "case-by-case" analysis that applies several statutory factors to the factual circumstances of the use.[19]

Unauthorized use of a copyrighted work by a third party in a manner that implicates one of the copyright holder's exclusive rights constitutes infringement.[20] The copyright holder may file a lawsuit against an alleged infringer for a violation of any of the exclusive rights conferred by copyright. The Copyright Act provides several civil remedies to the copyright holder that is harmed by infringement, including the possibility of obtaining injunctive relief,[21] actual damages suffered by the copyright owner due to the infringement,[22] statutory damages,[23] and costs and attorney fees.[24]

As noted above, the rights conferred on a copyright holder do not last forever. In general, an author of a creative work may enjoy copyright protection for the work for a term lasting the entirety of his/her life plus 70 additional years.[25] At the expiration of a term, the copyrighted work becomes part of the public domain. Materials that are in the public domain are available for anyone to reproduce, display, adapt, distribute, or publicly perform, without needing to obtain prior permission of the author or creator of such work.

Intellectual Property Treaties: Berne Convention and TRIPS

A widely cited author of a copyright treatise, David Nimmer, has explained that "[f]or decades, the outstanding feature distinguishing United States copyright law from that of the rest of the world has been its emphasis on formalities."[26] Historically, federal copyright law required creators of works to satisfy certain statutory formalities in order to obtain and maintain copyright protection, including providing notice on the published work (affixing to the work the © symbol, the word "Copyright," and the name of the owner of the copyright and the first year of the work's publication), depositing copies of the work with the U.S. Copyright Office (thus expanding the collection of the Library of Congress), and filing a registration form with the Copyright Office. If a creator of a work failed to meet the formalities, it could result in either a loss of copyright (the work thus falling into the public domain), preclude copyright protection, or restrict certain remedies under the copyright.[27]

In 1989, the United States became signatory to the Berne Convention for the Protection of Literary and Artistic Works of 1886. The Berne Convention sets certain minimum standards for copyright protection in member countries and requires each signatory country to afford the same copyright protections to authors in other member countries that it provides to its own authors. Article 5(2) of the Convention prohibits signatory countries from subjecting the "enjoyment and exercise" of copyright rights "to any formality."[28] In order to satisfy this requirement, the United States eliminated all the formalities in the Copyright Act that acted as conditions to copyright protection[29] by enacting the Berne Convention Implementation Act (BCIA) of 1988.[30]

In addition, article 18 of the Berne Convention specifies that "[t]his Convention shall apply to all works which, at the moment of its coming into force, have not yet fallen into the public domain in the country of origin through the expiry of the term of protection."[31] Thus, the United States appeared to be obliged by Berne to provide copyright protection for works authored by nationals of signatory countries that were in the U.S. public domain not on account of their expired copyright term, but because they had not satisfied the procedural formalities to secure copyright protection that the Copyright Act had required at that time. However, the BCIA did not extend copyrights to any of these foreign works.[32]

In April 1994, the United States and 123 other countries negotiated various agreements in the Uruguay Round of Multilateral Trade Negotiations, that concluded with the signing of the Marrakesh Agreement Establishing the World Trade Organization (WTO Agreement).[33] One of the agreements included in the Uruguay Round was the Agreement on Trade-Related Aspects of Intellectual Property Rights ("TRIPS Agreement"), which establishes minimum standards of protection for patents, copyrights, trademarks, and trade secrets that each WTO signatory state must give to the intellectual property of fellow WTO members.[34] Article 9(1) of TRIPS specifies that "Members shall comply with Articles 1 through 21 of the Berne Convention"[35] which includes article 18, the requirement to restore copyright protection for certain foreign works. Unlike the Berne Convention, the TRIPS Agreement provides for dispute resolution proceedings before the WTO, meaning that a WTO member found not to be in compliance with the TRIPS Agreement could be subject to trade sanctions.[36]

Section 514 of the Uruguay Round Agreements Act of 1994

To implement the agreements that the United States signed in the Uruguay Round, Congress enacted the Uruguay Round Agreements Act (URAA) in 1994.[37] Section 514 of URAA satisfies the United States' treaty obligations under article 18 of Berne and article 9(1) of TRIPS by granting copyright protection to foreign works that were formerly in the U.S. public domain because, among other things, their creators never obtained copyright protection in the United States or they lost such protection due to a failure to comply with statutory formalities.[38] However, § 514 of URAA did not restore copyrights in foreign works that entered the public domain due to an expiration of their term of protection.[39] The restored copyrights "subsist for the remainder of the term of copyright that the work would have otherwise been granted ... if the work never entered the public domain."[40] According to the former Register of Copyrights Marybeth Peters, the effect of § 514 of the URAA was to remove millions of foreign works from the public domain.[41]

Eldred v. Ashcroft

In 1998, Congress passed the Sony Bono Copyright Term Extension Act (CTEA)[42] that added 20 years to the term of copyright for both subsisting and future copyrights, in order to bring U.S. copyright terms more closely into conformance with those governed by the European Union. Hence, the law currently provides that an author of a creative work may enjoy copyright protection for the work for a term lasting the entirety of his/her life plus 70 additional years.

Plaintiffs representing individuals and businesses that rely upon and utilize materials in the public domain filed a lawsuit against the U.S. Attorney General to obtain a declaration that the CTEA was unconstitutional. Among other things, the plaintiffs argued that in extending the term of subsisting copyrights, the CTEA violated the "limited Times" requirement of the Copyright Clause. The lower court held in favor of the Attorney General, finding no constitutional problems.[43] The U.S. Court of Appeals for the District of Columbia Circuit affirmed the district court.[44]

Justice Ginsburg wrote the majority opinion in *Eldred v. Ashcroft*,[45] in which the Court upheld the CTEA by a vote of 7-2.[46] She stated that "[h]istory reveals an unbroken congressional practice of granting to authors the benefit of term extensions so that all under copyright protection will be governed evenhandedly under the same regime."[47] She rejected the plaintiffs' argument that the "limited Times" requirement requires a forever "fixed" or "inalterable" copyright term.[48] Ultimately, the Court found that the unbroken congressional practice for over two centuries of applying adjustments to copyright term to both existing and future works "is almost conclusive."[49]

However, the *Eldred* Court appeared to leave open the door to a future First Amendment challenge brought against an act of Congress that "alter[s] the traditional contours of copyright protection":

> The First Amendment securely protects the freedom to make—or decline to make – one's own speech; it bears less heavily when speakers assert the right to make other people's speeches. To the extent such assertions raise First Amendment concerns, copyright's built-in free speech safeguards are generally adequate to address them. We recognize that the D. C. Circuit spoke too broadly when it declared copyrights "categorically immune from challenges under the First Amendment." But when, as in this case, Congress has not altered the traditional contours of copyright protection, further First Amendment scrutiny is unnecessary.[50]

LEGAL ANALYSIS OF *GOLAN V. HOLDER*

Factual Background

Similar to the plaintiffs in *Eldred,* the plaintiffs in *Golan v. Holder* are orchestra conductors, educators, performers, publishers, film archivists, and motion picture distributors who rely on the free availability of artistic works in the public domain for their livelihoods.[51] One of the plaintiffs, Lawrence Golan, performs and teaches works by foreign composers including Dmitri Shostakovich and Igor Stravinsky. Prior to the enactment of the URAA, the plaintiffs used or performed works by foreign artists in the public domain such as Sergei Prokofiev's "Peter and the Wolf."[52] Because § 514 of the URAA restored copyright protection to these foreign works and many others that had previously been in the public domain, the "plaintiffs are either prevented from using these works or are required to pay licensing fees to the copyright holders—fees that are often cost-prohibitive for plaintiffs."[53]

In 2001, the plaintiffs filed a lawsuit challenging the constitutionality of § 514 of the URAA as well as the Copyright Term Extension Act, arguing that both exceed Congress's powers under the Copyright Clause and that both violate the First Amendment.

Procedural History

In March 2004, the U.S. District Court for the District of Colorado granted the government's motion to dismiss the plaintiffs' challenge to the CTEA as it had been subsequently foreclosed by the Supreme Court's opinion in *Eldred v. Ashcroft.*[54] The district court also granted summary judgment to the government on the plaintiffs' two URAA claims, ruling that Congress had the power to enact § 514 of the URAA under the Copyright Clause and that the plaintiffs "had no protected interest in the now-copyrighted works."[55]

In 2007, the U.S. Court of Appeals for the Tenth Circuit affirmed the district court's dismissal of the CTEA claims and upheld the district court's conclusion that § 514 of the URAA did not exceed Congress's power under the Copyright Clause.[56] However, the Tenth Circuit Court of Appeals ruled that the plaintiffs "have shown sufficient free expression interests in works removed from the public domain to require First Amendment scrutiny of § 514."[57] The appellate court explained that "[b]ased on the *Eldred* Court's analysis, we examine the bedrock principle of copyright law that works in the public domain remain there and conclude that § 514 alters the traditional contours of copyright protection by deviating from this principle."[58] The appellate court then remanded the case to the district court to conduct a First Amendment review of the CTEA, to determine "whether § 514 is content-based or content-neutral," and to apply the appropriate level of constitutional scrutiny.[59]

On remand, the government and plaintiffs agreed that § 514 is a content-neutral regulation of speech that should be subject to intermediate scrutiny.[60] The district court granted the plaintiffs' motion for summary judgment, ruling that "to the extent Section 514 suppresses the right of reliance parties to use works they exploited while the works were in the public domain—Section 514 is substantially broader than necessary to achieve the Government's interest" in complying with the terms of the Berne Convention and is thus unconstitutional.[61]

In 2010, the U.S. Court of Appeals for the Tenth Circuit reversed the district court's judgment, finding that § 514 does not violate the First Amendment because it advances an important governmental interest and that it is not substantially broader than necessary to advance that interest.[62] The court explained that in order for an act of Congress to survive intermediate scrutiny, "the statute must be directed at an important or substantial governmental interest unrelated to the suppression of free expression."[63] The important governmental interest that the federal appellate court identified in this case was "protecting American copyright holders' interests abroad."[64] The court cited congressional testimony that described how "billions of dollars were being lost each year because foreign countries were not providing copyright protections to American works that were in the public domain abroad."[65] As the appellate court noted, § 514 of the URAA would alleviate these economic harms to U.S. copyright holders because, according to congressional testimony, "the United States' trading partners had represented that they would restore American copyrights only if the United States restored foreign copyrights."[66] The appellate court also ruled that § 514 is narrowly tailored to further this legitimate government interest.[67]

Arguments before the Supreme Court

The Supreme Court heared oral argument in *Golan v. Holder* on October 5, 2011. Justice Kagan recused herself from *Golan*.[68] Her recusal means that only eight justices considered the case; thus, it raises the possibility of a 4-4 tie vote, in which event the Tenth Circuit's three rulings regarding the constitutionality of § 514 would stand—(1) § 514 of the URAA did not exceed Congress's power under the Copyright Clause, (2) § 514 "alters the traditional contours of copyright protection" to require First Amendment scrutiny, and (3) § 514 does not violate the First Amendment because it advances an important governmental interest in securing greater protections for American authors abroad.

The petitioners (the plaintiffs in the case) argue that "[f]or two hundred years, copyright legislation was consistent with a simple command: what enters the public domain remains in the public domain," and that Congress, in enacting the Berne Convention Implementation Act, followed this tradition.[69] However, when Congress enacted the URAA, it "marked a startling and dramatic departure from the traditions of U.S. copyright law."[70] According to the petitioners, by removing works from the public domain, the URAA has violated the "limited Times" restriction of the Copyright Clause "by turning a fixed and predictable period into one that can be reset or resurrected at any time, even after it expires."[71] Furthermore, the URAA violates the First Amendment, the petitioners argue, because it "places substantial burdens on core speech and expression rights that once belonged to petitioners and other members of the American public."[72] Such burdens on the petitioners' speech rights are not justified by any important government interest, the petitioners assert.[73]

The U.S. Solicitor General submitted the government brief on the merits defending the constitutionality of § 514 of the URAA, arguing that Congress had the power to restore copyright protection to certain foreign works in the public domain and that the statute did not violate the First Amendment.[74]The government brief claims that § 514 is consistent with the text of the Copyright Clause that required copyrights to be issued for "limited times" because the term of protection for restored copyrights is limited.[75] In addition, the government asserts that historically, Congress has "granted copyright protection to a substantial range of pre-existing works that had previously been open to public exploitation,[76] citing, for example, the first federal copyright statute enacted by the First Congress in 1790 that had conferred copyright protection to "any map, chart, book or books already printed within these United States."[77]

The government also defends § 514 as consistent with the First Amendment and argues that § 514 "should be reviewed under the deferential rational-basis standard that generally applies to Copyright Clause legislation."[78] On this point, the government refutes the Tenth Circuit's holding (in its ruling on the initial appeal of this case) that the statute alters the "traditional contours of copyright protection" and thus deserves heightened First Amendment scrutiny:[79]

> [T]he Tenth Circuit misread that statement [by the Supreme Court in *Eldred*] to mandate a freestanding inquiry into whether particular copyright legislation alters any "traditional contour[]" or "timehonored tradition" of copyright protection. It also misread the historical record to find that "one of these traditional contours is the principle that once a work enters the public domain, no individual—not even the creator—may copyright it." That reading is inconsistent with *Eldred*, irreconcilable with established First Amendment doctrine, and unworkable in practice.[80]

The government brief claims that "[b]ecause Section 514 is a rational exercise of authority conferred on Congress by the Copyright Clause, and because the restrictions of which petitioners complain are simply inherent and traditional features of copyright protection, 'further First Amendment scrutiny is unnecessary.'"[81] Even if the Supreme Court finds that intermediate scrutiny is warranted for § 514, however, the government argues that § 514 furthers "at least three" important governmental interests unrelated to the suppression of free speech: (1) it ensures compliance with international obligations; (2) it secures greater protections for American authors abroad; and (3) it remedies historical inequalities in the copyright system.[82]

End Notes

[1] P.L. 103-465, § 514, 108 Stat. 4809, 4976-81 (1994) (codified as amended at 17 U.S.C. §§ 104A, 109).

[2] Golan v. Gonzales, 501 F.3d 1179, 1187 (10th Cir. 2007) ("Golan I").

[3] Golan v. Holder, 609 F.3d 1076, 1094 (10th Cir. 2010) ("Golan II").

[4] The Framers of the Constitution used the word "Science" to mean "learning or knowledge." Eldred v. Ashcroft, 537 U.S. 186, 243 (2003) (Breyer, J., dissenting).

[5] U.S. CONST. art. I, § 8, cl. 8.

[6] Feist Publ'ns, Inc. v. Rural Tel. Serv. Co., 499 U.S. 340, 349 (1991) (*quoting* U.S. CONST. art. I, § 8, cl. 8.)

[7] "Original" means that the author must have independently created the work, as opposed to copying something from a pre-existing work. In addition, an "original work" must possess a minimal amount of creativity. Feist Publications, Inc. v. Rural Telephone Service Company, Inc., 499 U.S. 340, 345 (1991).

[8] 17 U.S.C. § 102(a).

[9] 17 U.S.C. § 201(a).

[10] 17 U.S.C. § 201(d).

[11] Baker v. Selden, 101 U.S. 99 (1879); 17 U.S.C. § 102(b).

[12] 17 U.S.C. § 106. For a detailed description of the major provisions of the Copyright Act, *see* CRS Report RS22801, *General Overview of U.S. Copyright Law*, by Brian T. Yeh.

[13] 17 U.S.C. §§ 201(d), 204(a).

[14] 17 U.S.C. § 109(a).

[15] 17 U.S.C. § 108.

[16] 17 U.S.C. § 110(3).

[17] 17 U.S.C. § 110(4).

[18] 17 U.S.C. § 107.

[19] Campbell v. Acuff-Rose Music, Inc., 510 U.S. 569, 577 (1994).

[20] 17 U.S.C. § 501.

[21] 17 U.S.C. § 502.

[22] 17 U.S.C. § 504(b).

[23] 17 U.S.C. § 504(c)(1).

[24] 17 U.S.C. § 505.

[25] 17 U.S.C. § 302. Other terms have been established for different works and different periods of time. For a concise chart explaining the different terms, *see* http://www.copyright. cornell.edu/resources/publicdomain.cfm.

[26] 2-7 M. NIMMER & D. NIMMER, NIMMER ON COPYRIGHT § 7.01 (2011).

[27] Id.

[28] Berne Convention for the Protection of Literary and Artistic Works of 1886, art. 5(2), available at http://www.wipo.int/treaties

[29] 4-17 M. NIMMER & D. NIMMER, NIMMER ON COPYRIGHT § 17.01 (2011).

[30] P.L. 100-568, 102 Stat. 2853 (1988).

[31] Berne Convention for the Protection of Literary and Artistic Works of 1886, art. 18, available at http://www.wipo.int/treaties

[32] See P.L. 100-568, § 12, 102 Stat. 2853, 2860 (1988) ("Title 17, United States Code, as amended by this Act, does not provide copyright protection for any work that is in the public domain in the United States.").

[33] For more information about the WTO, *see* CRS Report RS22154, *World Trade Organization (WTO) Decisions and Their Effect in U.S. Law*, by Jeanne J. Grimmett.

[34] World Trade Organization, Understanding the WTO - Intellectual Property: Protection and Enforcement, *at* http://www.wto.org/english/thewto_e/whatis_e/tif_e/agrm7_e.htm. Compliance with TRIPS is a prerequisite for WTO membership.

[35] Agreement on Trade-Related Aspects of Intellectual Property Rights, art. 9(1), *available at* http://www.wto.org/ english/tratop_e/trips_e/t_agm3_e.htm.

[36] For more information on this topic, *see* CRS Report RS20088, *Dispute Settlement in the World Trade Organization (WTO): An Overview*, by Jeanne J. Grimmett.

[37] P.L. 103-465, 108 Stat. 4809.

[38] Golan v. Holder, 609 F.3d 1076, 1081 (10th Cir. 2010) ("Golan II").

[39] 17 U.S.C. § 104A(h)(6)(B).

[40] 17 U.S.C. § 104A(a)(1)(B).

[41] Marybeth Peters, *The Year in Review: Accomplishments and Objectives of the U.S. Copyright Office,* 7 FORDHAM INTELL. PROP. MEDIA & ENT. L.J. 25, 31 (1996).

[42] P.L. 105-298, 112 Stat. 2827.

[43] Eldred v. Reno, 74 F. Supp.2d 1 (D.D.C. 1999).

[44] Eldred v. Reno, 239 F.3d 372, 373 (D.C.Cir. 2001).

[45] 537 U.S. 186 (2003).

[46] For a more thorough analysis of this case, *see* CRS Report RS21179, *Copyright Term Extension: Eldred v. Ashcroft*, by Robin Jeweler.

[47] *Eldred,* 537 U.S. at 200.

[48] *Id.* at 199.

[49] *Id.* (citation omitted).

[50] *Id.* at 221 (citation omitted).

[51] *Golan II,* 609 F.3d at 1081-82.

[52] Golan v. Gonzales, 501 F.3d 1179, 1182 (10th Cir. 2007) ("Golan I").

[53] *Golan II,* 609 F.3d at 1082.

[54] Golan v. Ashcroft, 310 F. Supp. 2d 1215, 1218 (D. Colo. 2004).

[55] *Golan I,* 501 F.3d at 1183.

[56] *Id.* at 1182.

[57] *Id.*

[58] *Id.* at 1187-88.

[59] *Id.* at 1196.

[60] *Golan II,* 609 F.3d at 1082; for more information on the standards that courts apply in a First Amendment analysis of a government regulation of speech, *see* CRS Report 95-815, *Freedom of Speech and Press: Exceptions to the First Amendment*, by Kathleen Ann Ruane ("If the government limits speech, but its purpose in doing so is not based on the content of the speech, then the limitation on speech may still violate the First Amendment, but it is less likely than a content-based restriction to do so. This is because the Supreme Court applies less than 'strict scrutiny' to non-contentbased restrictions. With respect to non-content-based restrictions, the Court requires that the governmental interest be 'significant' or 'substantial' or 'important,' but not necessarily, as with content-based restrictions, 'compelling.' And, in the case of non-content-based restrictions, the Court requires that the restriction be narrowly tailored, but not, as with content-based restrictions, that it be the least restrictive means to advance the governmental interest.").

[61] Golan v. Holder, 611 F. Supp. 2d 1165, 1177 (D. Colo. 2009).

[62] *Golan II,* 609 F.3d at 1080, 1083.

[63] *Id.* at 1083, *citing* Turner Broad. Sys., Inc. v. FCC, 512 U.S. 622, 662 (1994) ("Turner I").

[64] *Id.* at 1083.

[65] *Id.* at 1086 (citations omitted).

[66] *Id.* at 1087 (citations omitted).

[67] *Id.* at 1090-91.

[68] Lyle Denniston, *A Major Test of Copyright Power,* SCOTUSBLOG.COM, March 7, 2011.

[69] Brief for the Petitioners at 3, Golan v. Holder, No. 10-545.

[70] *Id.* at 14-15.

[71] *Id.* at 15-16.

[72] *Id.* at 17.

[73] *Id.* ("[T]here is no legitimate interest in giving away public speech rights in the hope of creating private economic windfalls.").

[74] Brief for the Respondents, Golan v. Holder, No. 10-545.

[75] *Id.* at 10-11.

[76] *Id.* at 11.

[77] *Id.* at 18 (citation omitted).

[78] *Id.* at 42.

[79] *Id.* at 12.

[80] *Id.* at 35.

[81] *Id.* at 34, *quoting Eldred,* 537 U.S. at 221.
[82] *Id.* at 42-43.

In: Copyright Restoration…
Editors: N. Hernandez, A. King

ISBN: 978-1-62081-174-0

Chapter 2

SUPREME COURT OF THE UNITED STATES*†

Golan et al. V. Holder, Attorney General, et al.

Certiorari to the United States Court
of Appeals for the Tenth Circuit
No. 10–545. Argued October 5, 2011—
Decided January 18, 2012

SYLLABUS

The Berne Convention for the Protection of Literary and Artistic Works (Berne), which took effect in 1886, is the principal accord governing international copyright relations. Berne's 164 member states agree to provide a minimum level of copyright protection and to treat authors from other member countries as well as they treat their own. Of central importance in this case,

† NOTE: Where it is feasible, a syllabus (headnote) will be released, as is being done in connection with this case, at the time the opinion is issued. The syllabus constitutes no part of the opinion of the Court but has been prepared by the Reporter of Decisions for the convenience of the reader. See United States v. Detroit Timber & Lumber Co., 200 U. S. 321, 337.

* This is an edited, reformatted and augmented version of Supreme Court document, dated October, 2011.

Article 18 of Berne requires countries to protect the works of other member states unless the works' copyright term has expired in either the country where protection is claimed or the country of origin. A different system of transnational copyright protection long prevailed in this country. Throughout most of the 20th century, the only foreign authors eligible for Copyright Act protection were those whose countries granted reciprocal rights to American authors and whose works were printed in the United States. Despite Article 18, when the United States joined Berne in 1989, it did not protect any foreign works lodged in the U. S. public domain, many of them works never protected here. In 1994, however, the Agreement on Trade-Related Aspects of Intellectual Property Rights mandated implementation of Berne's first 21 articles, on pain of enforcement by the World Trade Organization.

In response, Congress applied the term of protection available to U. S. works to preexisting works from Berne member countries. Section 514 of the Uruguay Round Agreements Act (URAA) grants copyright protection to works protected in their country of origin, but lacking protection in the United States for any of three reasons: The United States did not protect works from the country of origin at the time of publication; the United States did not protect sound recordings fixed before 1972; or the author had not complied with certain U. S. statutory formalities. Works encompassed by §514 are granted the protection they would have enjoyed had the United States maintained copyright relations with the author's country or removed formalities incompatible with Berne. As a consequence of the barriers to U. S. copyright protection prior to §514's enactment, foreign works "restored" to protection by the measure had entered the public domain in this country. To cushion the impact of their placement in protected status, §514 provides ameliorating accommodations for parties who had exploited affected works before the URAA was enacted.

Petitioners are orchestra conductors, musicians, publishers, and others who formerly enjoyed free access to works §514 removed from the public domain. They maintain that Congress, in passing §514, exceeded its authority under the Copyright Clause and transgressed First Amendment limitations. The District Court granted the Attorney General's motion for summary judgment. Affirming in part, the Tenth Circuit agreed that Congress had not offended the Copyright Clause, but concluded that §514 required further First Amendment inspection in light of *Eldred* v. *Ashcroft*, 537 U. S. 186. On remand, the District Court granted summary judgment to petitioners on the First Amendment claim, holding that §514's constriction of the public domain was not justified by any of the asserted federal interests. The Tenth Circuit reversed, ruling that §514 was narrowly tailored to fit the important government aim of protecting U. S. copyright holders' interests abroad.

Held:

1. Section 514 does not exceed Congress' authority under the Copyright Clause. Pp. 13–23.

(a) The text of the Copyright Clause does not exclude application of copyright protection to works in the public domain. *Eldred* is largely dispositive of petitioners' claim that the Clause's confinement of a copyright's lifespan to a "limited Tim[e]" prevents the removal of works from the public domain. In *Eldred,* the Court upheld the Copyright Term Extension Act (CTEA), which extended, by 20 years, the terms of existing copyrights. The text of the Copyright Clause, the Court observed, contains no "command that a time prescription, once set, becomes forever 'fixed' or 'inalterable,' " and the Court declined to infer any such command. 537 U. S., at 199. The construction petitioners tender here is similarly infirm. The terms afforded works restored by §514 are no less "limited" than those the CTEA lengthened. Nor had the "limited Tim[e]" already passed for the works at issue here—many of them works formerly denied any U. S. copyright protection—for a period of exclusivity must begin before it may end. Petitioners also urge that the Government's position would allow Congress to legislate perpetual copyright terms by instituting successive "limited" terms as prior terms expire. But as in *Eldred*, such hypothetical misbehavior is far afield from this case. In aligning the United States with other nations bound by Berne, Congress can hardly be charged with a design to move stealthily toward a perpetual copyright regime. Pp. 13–15.

(b) Historical practice corroborates the Court's reading of the Copyright Clause to permit the protection of previously unprotected works. In the Copyright Act of 1790, the First Congress protected works that had been freely reproducible under State copyright laws. Subsequent actions confirm that Congress has not understood the Copyright Clause to preclude protection for existing works. Several private bills restored the copyrights and patents of works and inventions previously in the public domain. Congress has also passed generally applicable legislation granting copyrights and patents to works and inventions that had lost protection. Pp. 15–19.

(c) Petitioners also argue that §514 fails to "promote the Progress of Science" as contemplated by the initial words of the Copyright Clause. Specifically, they claim that because §514 affects only works already created, it cannot meet the Clause's objective. The creation of new works, however, is not the sole way Congress may promote "Science," *i.e.,* knowledge and learning. In *Eldred*, this Court rejected a nearly identical argument, concluding that the Clause does not demand that each copyright provision, examined discretely, operate to induce new works. Rather the Clause "empowers Congress to determine the intellectual property regimes that, overall, in that body's judgment, will serve the ends of the Clause." 537 U. S., at 222. Nothing in the text or history of the Copyright Clause, moreover, confines the "Progress of Science" exclusively to "incentives for creation." Historical evidence, congressional practice, and this Court's decisions, in fact, suggest that inducing the dissemination of existing works is an appropriate means to promote science. Pp. 20–22.

(d) Considered against this backdrop, §514 falls comfortably within Congress' Copyright Clause authority. Congress had reason to believe that a well-functioning international copyright system would encourage the dissemination of existing and future works. And testimony informed Congress that full compliance with Berne would expand the foreign markets available to U. S. authors and invigorate protection against piracy of U. S. works abroad, thus benefitting copyright-intensive industries stateside and inducing greater investment in the creative process. This Court has no warrant to reject Congress' rational judgment that exemplary adherence to Berne would serve the objectives of the Copyright Clause. Pp. 22–23.

2. The First Amendment does not inhibit the restoration authorized by §514. Pp. 23–32.

(a) The pathmarking *Eldred* decision is again instructive. There, the Court held that the CTEA's enlargement of a copyright's duration did not offend the First Amendment's freedom of expression guarantee. Recognizing that some restriction on expression is the inherent and intended effect of every grant of copyright, the Court observed that the Framers regarded copyright protection not simply as a limit on the manner in which expressive works may be used, but also as an "engine of free expression." 537 U. S., at 219. The "traditional contours" of copyright protection, *i.e.*, the "idea/expression dichotomy" and the "fair use" defense, moreover, serve as "built-in First Amendment accommodations." *Ibid.* Given the speech-protective purposes and safeguards embraced by copyright law, there was no call for the heightened review sought in *Eldred.* The Court reaches the same conclusion here. Section 514 leaves undisturbed the idea/expression distinction and the fair use defense. Moreover, Congress adopted measures to ease the transition from a national scheme to an international copyright regime. Pp. 23–26.

(b) Petitioners claim that First Amendment interests of a higher order are at stake because they—unlike their *Eldred* counterparts— enjoyed "vested rights" in works that had already entered the public domain. Their contentions depend on an argument already considered and rejected, namely, that the Constitution renders the public domain largely untouchable by Congress. Nothing in the historical record, subsequent congressional practice, or this Court's jurisprudence warrants exceptional First Amendment solicitude for copyrighted works that were once in the public domain. Congress has several times adjusted copyright law to protect new categories of works as well as works previously in the public domain. Section 514, moreover, does not impose a blanket prohibition on public access. The question is whether would-be users of certain foreign works must pay for their desired use of the author's expression, or else limit their exploitation to "fair use" of those works. By fully implementing Berne, Congress ensured that these works, like domestic and most other foreign works, would be governed by the same legal regime. Section 514 simply placed foreign works in the position they would have occupied if the current copyright regime had been in effect when those works were created and first published. Pp. 26–30.

609 F. 3d 1076, affirmed.

GINSBURG, J., delivered the opinion of the Court, in which ROBERTS, C. J., and SCALIA, KENNEDY, THOMAS, and SOTOMAYOR, JJ., joined. BREYER, J., filed a dissenting opinion, in which ALITO, J., joined. KAGAN, J., took no part in the consideration or decision of the case.

SUPREME COURT OF THE UNITED STATES†

Lawrence Golan, et al., Petitioners V. Eric H. Holder, Jr., Attorney General, et al.

No. 10–545

On Writ of Certiorari to the United States Court of Appeals for the Tenth Circuit [January 18, 2012]

Justice Ginsburg delivered the opinion of the Court.

† NOTICE: This opinion is subject to formal revision before publication in the preliminary print of the United States Reports. Readers are requested to notify the Reporter of Decisions, Supreme Court of the United States, Washington, D. C. 20543, of any typographical or other formal errors, in order that corrections may be made before the preliminary print goes to press.

The Berne Convention for the Protection of Literary and Artistic Works (Berne Convention or Berne), which took effect in 1886, is the principal accord governing international copyright relations. Latecomer to the international copyright regime launched by Berne, the United States joined the Convention in 1989. To perfect U. S. implementation of Berne, and as part of our response to the Uruguay Round of multilateral trade negotiations, Congress, in 1994, gave works enjoying copyright protection abroad the same full term of protection available to U. S. works. Congress did so in §514 of the Uruguay Round Agreements Act (URAA), which grants copyright protection to preexisting works of Berne member countries, protected in their country of origin, but lacking protection in the United States for any of three reasons: The United States did not protect works from the country of origin at the time of publication; the United States did not protect sound recordings fixed before 1972; or the author had failed to comply with U. S. statutory formalities (formalities Congress no longer requires as prerequisites to copyright protection).

The URAA accords no protection to a foreign work after its full copyright term has expired, causing it to fall into the public domain, whether under the laws of the country of origin or of this country. Works encompassed by §514 are granted the protection they would have enjoyed had the United States maintained copyright relations with the author's country or removed formalities incompatible with Berne. Foreign authors, however, gain no credit for the protection they lacked in years prior to §514's enactment. They therefore enjoy fewer total years of exclusivity than do their U. S. counterparts. As a consequence of the barriers to U. S. copyright protection prior to the enactment of §514, foreign works "restored" to protection by the measure had entered the public domain in this country. To cushion the impact of their placement in protected status, Congress included in §514 ameliorating accommodations for parties who had exploited affected works before the URAA was enacted.

Petitioners include orchestra conductors, musicians, publishers, and others who formerly enjoyed free access to works §514 removed from the public domain. They maintain that the Constitution's Copyright and Patent Clause, Art. I, §8, cl. 8, and First Amendment both decree the invalidity of §514. Under those prescriptions of our highest law, petitioners assert, a work that has entered the public domain, for whatever reason, must forever remain there.

In accord with the judgment of the Tenth Circuit, we conclude that §514 does not transgress constitutional limitations on Congress' authority. Neither the Copyright and Patent Clause nor the First Amendment, we hold, makes the public domain, in any and all cases, a territory that works may never exit.

I

A

Members of the Berne Union agree to treat authors from other member countries as well as they treat their own.

Berne Convention, Sept. 9, 1886, as revised at Stockholm on July 14, 1967, Art. 1, 5(1), 828 U. N. T. S. 221, 225, 231–233. Nationals of a member country, as well as any author who publishes in one of Berne's 164 member states, thus enjoy copyright protection in nations across the globe. Art. 2(6), 3. Each country, moreover, must afford at least the minimum level of protection specified by Berne. The copyright term must span the author's lifetime, plus at least 50 additional years, whether or not the author has complied with a member state's legal formalities. Art. 5(2), 7(1). And, as relevant here, a work must be protected abroad unless its copyright term has expired in either the country where protection is claimed or the country of origin. Art. 18(1)–(2).[1]

A different system of transnational copyright protection long prevailed in this country. Until 1891, foreign works were categorically excluded from Copyright Act protection. Throughout most of the 20th century, the only eligible foreign authors were those whose countries granted reciprocal rights to U. S. authors and whose works were printed in the United States. See Act of Mar. 3, 1891, §3, 13, 26 Stat. 1107, 1110; Patry, The United States and International Copyright Law, 40 Houston L. Rev. 749, 750 (2003).[2] For domestic and foreign authors alike, protection hinged on compliance with notice, registration, and renewal formalities.

The United States became party to Berne's multilateral, formality-free copyright regime in 1989. Initially, Congress adopted a "minimalist approach" to compliance with the Convention. H. R. Rep. No. 100–609, p. 7 (1988) (hereinafter BCIA House Report). The Berne Convention Implementation Act of 1988 (BCIA), 102 Stat. 2853, made "only those changes to American copyright law that [were] clearly required under the treaty's provisions," BCIA House Report, at 7. Despite Berne's instruction that member countries—including "new accessions to the Union"— protect foreign works under copyright in the country of origin, Art. 18(1) and (4), 828 U. N. T. S., at 251, the BCIA accorded no protection for "any work that is in the public domain in the United States," §12, 102 Stat. 2860. Protection of future foreign works, the BCIA indicated, satisfied Article 18. See §2(3), 102 Stat. 2853

("The amendments made by this Act, together with the law as it exists on the date of the enactment of this Act, satisfy the obligations of the United States in adhering to the Berne Convention …"). Congress indicated, however, that it had not definitively rejected "retroactive" protection for preexisting foreign works; instead it had punted on this issue of Berne's implementation, deferring consideration until "a more thorough examination of Constitutional, commercial, and consumer considerations is possible." BCIA House Report, at 51, 52.[3]

The minimalist approach essayed by the United States did not sit well with other Berne members.[4] While negotiations were ongoing over the North American Free Trade Agreement (NAFTA), Mexican authorities complained about the United States' refusal to grant protection, in accord with Article 18, to Mexican works that remained under copyright domestically. See Intellectual Property and International Issues, Hearings before the Subcommittee on Intellectual Property and Judicial Administration, House Committee on the Judiciary, 102d Cong., 1st Sess., 168 (1991) (statement of Ralph Oman, U. S. Register of Copyrights).[5] The Register of Copyrights also reported "questions" from Turkey, Egypt, and Austria. *Ibid.* Thailand and Russia balked at protecting U. S. works, copyrighted here but in those countries' public domains, until the United States reciprocated with respect to their authors' works. URAA Joint Hearing 137 (statement of Ira S. Shapiro, General Counsel, Office of the U. S. Trade Representative (USTR)); *id.*, at 208 (statement of Professor Shira Perlmutter); *id.*, at 291 (statement of Jason S. Berman, Recording Industry Association of America (RIAA)).[6]

Berne, however, did not provide a potent enforcement mechanism. The Convention contemplates dispute resolution before the International Court of Justice. Art. 33(1). But it specifies no sanctions for noncompliance and allows parties, at any time, to declare themselves "not … bound" by the Convention's dispute resolution provision. Art. 33(2)–(3) 828 U. N. T. S., at 277. Unsurprisingly, no enforcement actions were launched before 1994. D. Gervais, The TRIPS Agreement 213, and n. 134 (3d ed. 2008). Although "several Berne Union Members disagreed with [our] interpretation of Article 18," the USTR told Congress, the Berne Convention did "not provide a meaningful dispute resolution process." URAA Joint Hearing 137 (statement of Shapiro). This shortcoming left Congress "free to adopt a minimalist approach and evade Article 18." Karp, Final Report, Berne Article 18 Study on Retroactive United States Copyright Protection for Berne and other Works, 20 Colum.-VLA J. L. & Arts 157, 172 (1996).

The landscape changed in 1994. The Uruguay round of multilateral trade negotiations produced the World Trade Organization (WTO) and the Agreement on Trade-Related Aspects of Intellectual Property Rights (TRIPS).[7] The United States joined both. TRIPS mandates, on pain of WTO enforcement, implementation of Berne's first 21 articles. TRIPS, Art. 9.1, 33 I. L. M. 1197, 1201 (requiring adherence to all but the "moral rights" provisions of Article 6*bis*). The WTO gave teeth to the Convention's requirements: Noncompliance with a WTO ruling could subject member countries to tariffs or cross-sector retaliation. See Gervais, *supra*, at 213; 7 W. Patry, Copyright §24:1, pp. 24–8 to 24–9 (2011). The specter of WTO enforcement proceedings bolstered the credibility of our trading partners' threats to challenge the United States for inadequate compliance with Article 18. See URAA Joint Hearing 137 (statement of Shapiro, USTR) ("It is likely that other WTO members would challenge the current U. S. implementation of Berne Article 18 under [WTO] procedures.").[8]

Congress' response to the Uruguay agreements put to rest any questions concerning U. S. compliance with Article 18. Section 514 of the URAA, 108 Stat. 4976 (codified at 17 U. S. C. §104A, 109(a)),[9] extended copyright to works that garnered protection in their countries of origin,[10] but had no right to exclusivity in the United States for any of three reasons: lack of copyright relations between the country of origin and the United States at the time of publication; lack of subject-matter protection for sound recordings fixed before 1972; and failure to comply with U. S. statutory formalities (*e.g.*, failure to provide notice of copyright status, or to register and renew a copyright). See §104A(h)(6)(B)–(C).[11]

Works that have fallen into the public domain after the expiration of a full copyright term—either in the United States or the country of origin—receive no further protection under §514. *Ibid.*[12] Copyrights "restored"[13] under URAA §514 "subsist for the remainder of the term of copyright that the work would have otherwise been granted … if the work never entered the public domain." §104A(a)(1)(B). Prospectively, restoration places foreign works on an equal footing with their U. S. counterparts; assuming a foreign and domestic author died the same day, their works will enter the public domain simultaneously. See §302(a) (copyrights generally expire 70 years after the author's death). Restored works, however, receive no compensatory time for the period of exclusivity they would have enjoyed before §514's enactment, had they been protected at the outset in the United States. Their total term, therefore, falls short of that available to similarly situated U. S. works.

The URAA's disturbance of the public domain hardly escaped Congress' attention. Section 514 imposed no liability for any use of foreign works occurring before restoration. In addition, anyone remained free to copy and use restored works for one year following §514's enactment. See 17 U. S. C. §104A(h)(2)(A). Concerns about §514's compatibility with the Fifth Amendment's Takings Clause led Congress to include additional protections for "reliance parties"—those who had, before the URAA's enactment, used or acquired a foreign work then in the public domain. See §104A(h)(3)–(4).[14] Reliance parties may continue to exploit a restored work until the owner of the restored copyright gives notice of intent to enforce— either by filing with the U. S. Copyright Office within two years of restoration, or by actually notifying the reliance party. §104A(c), (d)(2)(A)(i), and (B)(i). After that, reliance parties may continue to exploit existing copies for a grace period of one year. §104A(d)(2)(A)(ii), and (B)(ii). Finally, anyone who, before the URAA's enactment, created a "derivative work" based on a restored work may indefinitely exploit the derivation upon payment to the copyright holder of "reasonable compensation," to be set by a district judge if the parties cannot agree. §104A(d)(3).

B

In 2001, petitioners filed this lawsuit challenging §514. They maintain that Congress, when it passed the URAA, exceeded its authority under the Copyright Clause and transgressed First Amendment limitations.[15] The District Court granted the Attorney General's motion for summary judgment. *Golan* v. *Gonzales*, No. Civ. 01–B–1854, 2005 WL 914754 (D. Colo., Apr. 20, 2005). In rejecting petitioners' Copyright Clause argument, the court stated that Congress "has historically demonstrated little compunction about removing copyrightable materials from the public domain." *Id.*, at *14. The court next declined to part from "the settled rule that private censorship via copyright enforcement does not implicate First Amendment concerns." *Id.*, at *17.

The Court of Appeals for the Tenth Circuit affirmed in part. *Golan* v. *Gonzales*, 501 F. 3d 1179 (2007). The public domain, it agreed, was not a "threshold that Congress" was powerless to "traverse in both directions." *Id.*, at 1187 (internal quotations marks omitted). But §514, as the Court of Appeals read our decision in *Eldred* v. *Ashcroft*, 537 U. S. 186 (2003), required further First Amendment inspection, 501 F. 3d, at 1187. The measure "'altered the traditional contours of copyright protection,'" the court said—specifically, the "bedrock principle" that once works enter the public domain, they do not leave. *Ibid.* (quoting *Eldred*, 537 U. S., at 221). The case was remanded with an instruction to the District Court to address the First Amendment claim in light of the Tenth Circuit's opinion.

On remand, the District Court's starting premise was uncontested: Section 514 does not regulate speech on the basis of its content; therefore the law would be upheld if "narrowly tailored to serve a significant government interest." 611 F. Supp. 2d 1165, 1170–1171 (Colo. 2009) (quoting *Ward* v. *Rock Against Racism*, 491 U. S. 781, 791 (1989)). Summary judgment was due petitioners, the court concluded, because §514's constriction of the public domain was not justified by any of the asserted federal interests: compliance with Berne, securing greater protection for U. S. authors abroad, or remediation of the inequitable treatment suffered by foreign authors whose works lacked protection in the United States. 611 F. Supp. 2d, at 1172–1177.

The Tenth Circuit reversed. Deferring to Congress' predictive judgments in matters relating to foreign affairs, the appellate court held that §514 survived First Amendment scrutiny. Specifically, the court determined that the law was narrowly tailored to fit the important government aim of protecting U. S. copyright holders' interests abroad. 609 F. 3d 1076 (2010).

We granted certiorari to consider petitioners' challenge to §514 under both the Copyright Clause and the First Amendment, 562 U. S. ___ (2011), and now affirm.

II.

We first address petitioners' argument that Congress lacked authority, under the Copyright Clause, to enact §514. The Constitution states that "Congress shall have Power … [t]o promote the Progress of Science ... by securing for limited Times to Authors … the exclusive Right to their … Writings." Art. I, §8, cl. 8. Petitioners find in this grant of authority an impenetrable barrier to the extension of copyright protection to authors whose writings, for whatever reason, are in the public domain. We see no such barrier in the text of the Copyright Clause, historical practice, or our precedents.

A

The text of the Copyright Clause does not exclude application of copyright protection to works in the public domain. Symposium, Congressional Power and Limitations Inherent in the Copyright Clause, 30 Colum. J. L. & Arts 259, 266 (2007). Petitioners' contrary argument relies primarily on the Constitution's confinement of a copyright's lifespan to a "limited Tim[e]." "Removing works from the public domain," they contend, "violates the 'limited [t]imes' restriction by turning a fixed and predictable period into one that can be reset or resurrected at any time, even after it expires." Brief for Petitioners 22.

Our decision in *Eldred* is largely dispositive of petitioners' limited-time argument. There we addressed the question whether Congress violated the Copyright Clause when it extended, by 20 years, the terms of existing copyrights. 537 U. S., at 192–193 (upholding Copyright Term Extension Act (CTEA)). Ruling that Congress acted within constitutional bounds, we declined to infer from the text of the Copyright Clause "the command that a time prescription, once set, becomes forever 'fixed' or 'inalterable.'" *Id.,* at 199. "The word 'limited,' " we observed, "does not convey a meaning so constricted." *Ibid.* Rather, the term is best understood to mean "confine[d] within certain bounds," "restrain[ed]," or "circumscribed." *Ibid.* (internal quotation marks omitted). The construction petitioners tender closely resembles the definition rejected in *Eldred* and is similarly infirm.

The terms afforded works restored by §514 are no less "limited" than those the CTEA lengthened. In light of *Eldred*, petitioners do not here contend that the term Congress has granted U. S. authors—their lifetimes, plus 70 years—is unlimited. See 17 U. S. C. §302(a). Nor do petitioners explain why terms of the same duration, as applied to foreign works, are not equally "circumscribed" and "confined." See *Eldred*, 537 U. S., at 199. Indeed, as earlier noted, see *supra,* at 2, 10, the copyrights of restored foreign works typically last for fewer years than those of their domestic counterparts.

The difference, petitioners say, is that the limited time had already passed for works in the public domain. What was that limited term for foreign works once excluded from U. S. copyright protection? Exactly "zero," petitioners respond. Brief for Petitioners 22 (works in question "received a specific term of protection … sometimes expressly set to zero"; "at the end of that period," they "entered the public domain"); Tr. of Oral Arg. 52 (by "refusing to provide any protection for a work," Congress "set[s] the term at zero," and thereby "tell[s] us when the end has come"). We find scant sense in this argument, for surely a "limited time" of exclusivity must begin before it may end.[16]

Carried to its logical conclusion, petitioners persist, the Government's position would allow Congress to institute a second "limited" term after the first expires, a third after that, and so on. Thus, as long as Congress legislated in installments, perpetual copyright terms would be achievable. As in *Eldred*, the hypothetical legislative misbehavior petitioners posit is far afield from the case before us. See 537 U. S., at 198–200, 209–210. In aligning the United States with other nations bound by the Berne Convention, and thereby according equitable treatment to once disfavored foreign authors, Congress can hardly be charged with a design to move stealthily toward a regime of perpetual copyrights.

B

Historical practice corroborates our reading of the Copyright Clause to permit full U. S. compliance with Berne. Undoubtedly, federal copyright legislation generally has not affected works in the public domain. Section 514's disturbance of that domain, petitioners argue, distinguishes their suit from Eldred's. In adopting the CTEA, petitioners note, Congress acted in accord with "an unbroken congressional practice" of granting pre-expiration term extensions, 537 U. S., at 200. No comparable practice, they maintain, supports §514.

On occasion, however, Congress has seen fit to protect works once freely available. Notably, the Copyright Act of 1790 granted protection to many works previously in the public domain. Act of May 31, 1790 (1790 Act), §1, 1 Stat. 124 (covering "any map, chart, book, or books already printed within these United States"). Before the Act launched a uniform national system, three States provided no statutory copyright protection at all.[17] Of those that did afford some protection, seven failed to protect maps;[18] eight did not cover previously published books;[19] and all ten denied protection to works that failed to comply with formalities.[20] The First Congress, it thus appears, did not view the public domain as inviolate. As we have recognized, the "construction placed upon the Constitution by [the drafters of] the first [copyright] act of 1790 and the act of 1802 … men who were contemporary with [the Constitution's] formation, many of whom were members of the convention which framed it, is of itself entitled to very great weight." *Burrow-Giles Lithographic Co.* v. *Sarony*, 111 U. S. 53, 57 (1884).[21]

Subsequent actions confirm that Congress has not understood the Copyright Clause to preclude protection for existing works. Several private bills restored the copyrights of works that previously had been in the public domain. See Act of Feb. 19, 1849 (Corson Act), ch. 57, 9 Stat. 763; Act of June 23, 1874 (Helmuth Act), ch. 534, 18 Stat. 618; Act of Feb. 17, 1898 (Jones Act), ch. 29, 30 Stat. 1396. These bills were unchallenged in court.

Analogous patent statutes, however, were upheld in litigation.[22] In 1808, Congress passed a private bill restoring patent protection to Oliver Evans' flour mill. When Evans sued for infringement, first Chief Justice Marshall in the Circuit Court, *Evans* v. *Jordan*, 8 F. Cas. 872 (No. 4,564) (Va. 1813), and then Justice Bushrod Washington for this Court, *Evans* v. *Jordan*, 9 Cranch 199 (1815), upheld the restored patent's validity. After the patent's expiration, the Court said, "a general right to use [Evans'] discovery was not so vested in the public" as to allow the defendant to continue using the machinery, which he had constructed between the patent's expiration and the bill's passage. *Id.*, at 202. See also *Blanchard* v. *Sprague*, 3 F. Cas. 648, 650 (No. 1,518) (CC Mass. 1839) (Story, J.) ("I never have entertained any doubt of the constitutional authority of congress" to "give a patent for an invention, which … was in public use and enjoyed by the community at the time of the passage of the act.").

This Court again upheld Congress' restoration of an invention to protected status in *McClurg* v. *Kingsland*, 1 How. 202 (1843). There we enforced an 1839 amendment that recognized a patent on an invention despite its prior use by the inventor's employer. Absent such dispensation, the employer's use would have rendered the invention unpatentable, and therefore open to exploitation without the inventor's leave. *Id.*, at 206–209.

Congress has also passed generally applicable legislation granting patents and copyrights to inventions and works that had lost protection. An 1832 statute authorized a new patent for any inventor whose failure, "by inadvertence, accident, or mistake," to comply with statutory formalities rendered the original patent "invalid or inoperative." Act of July 3, §3, 4 Stat. 559. An 1893 measure similarly allowed authors who had not timely deposited their work to receive "all the rights and privileges" the Copyright Act affords, if they made the required deposit by March 1, 1893. Act of Mar. 3, ch. 215, 27 Stat. 743.[23] And in 1919 and 1941, Congress authorized the President to issue proclamations granting protection to foreign works that had fallen into the public domain during World Wars I and II. See Act of Dec. 18, 1919, ch. 11, 41 Stat. 368; Act of Sept. 25, 1941, ch. 421, 55 Stat. 732.[24]

Pointing to dictum in *Graham* v. *John Deere Co. of Kansas City*, 383 U. S. 1 (1966), petitioners would have us look past this history. In *Graham*, we stated that "Congress may not authorize the issuance of patents whose effects are to remove existent knowledge from the public domain, or to restrict free access to materials already available." *Id.*, at 6; *post*, at 15. But as we explained in *Eldred*, this passage did not speak to the constitutional limits on Congress' copyright and patent authority. Rather, it "addressed an invention's very eligibility for patent protection." 537 U. S., at 202, n. 7.

Installing a federal copyright system and ameliorating the interruptions of global war, it is true, presented Congress with extraordinary situations. Yet the TRIPS accord, leading the United States to comply in full measure with Berne, was also a signal event. See *supra,* at 7–8; cf. *Eldred*, 537 U. S., at 259, 264–265 (BREYER, J., dissenting) (acknowledging importance of international uniformity advanced by U. S. efforts to conform to the Berne Convention). Given the authority we hold Congress has, we will not second-guess the political choice Congress made between leaving the public domain untouched and embracing Berne unstintingly. Cf. *id.*, at 212–213.

C

Petitioners' ultimate argument as to the Copyright and Patent Clause concerns its initial words. Congress is empowered to "promote the Progress of Science and useful Arts" by enacting systems of copyright and patent protection. U. S. Const., Art. I, §8, cl. 8. Perhaps counterintuitively for the contemporary reader, Congress' copyright authority is tied to the progress of science; its patent authority, to the progress of the useful arts. See *Graham*, 383 U. S., at 5, and n. 1; *Evans*, 8 F. Cas., at 873 (Marshall, J.).

The "Progress of Science," petitioners acknowledge, refers broadly to "the creation and spread of knowledge and learning." Brief for Petitioners 21; accord *post*, at 1. They nevertheless argue that federal legislation cannot serve the Clause's aim unless the legislation "spur[s] the creation of … new works." Brief for Petitioners 24; accord *post*, at 1–2, 8, 17. Because §514 deals solely with works already created, petitioners urge, it "provides no plausible incentive to create new works" and is therefore invalid. Reply Brief 4.[25]

The creation of at least one new work, however, is not the sole way Congress may promote knowledge and learning. In *Eldred*, we rejected an argument nearly identical to the one petitioners rehearse. The *Eldred* petitioners urged that the "CTEA's extension of existing copyrights categorically fails to 'promote the Progress of Science,' … because it does not stimulate the creation of new works." 537 U. S., at 211–212. In response to this argument, we held that the Copyright Clause does not demand that each copyright provision, examined discretely, operate to induce new works. Rather, we explained, the Clause "empowers Congress to determine the intellectual property regimes that, overall, in that body's judgment, will serve the ends of the Clause." *Id.*, at 222. And those permissible ends, we held, extended beyond the creation of new works. See *id.*, at 205–206 (rejecting the notion that "'the only way to promote the progress of science [is] to provide incentives to create new works'" (quoting Perlmutter, Participation in the International Copyright System as a Means to Promote the Progress of Science and Useful Arts, 36 Loyola (LA) L. Rev. 323, 332 (2002))).[26]

Even were we writing on a clean slate, petitioners' argument would be unavailing. Nothing in the text of the Copyright Clause confines the "Progress of Science" exclusively to "incentives for creation." *Id.*, at 324, n. 5 (internal quotation marks omitted). Evidence from the founding, moreover, suggests that inducing *dissemination*—as opposed to creation—was viewed as an appropriate means to promote science. See Nachbar, Constructing Copyright's Mythology, 6 Green Bag 2d 37, 44 (2002) ("The scope of copyright protection existing at the time of the framing," trained as it was on "publication, not creation," "is inconsistent with claims that copyright must promote creative activity in order to be valid." (internal quotation marks omitted)). Until 1976, in fact, Congress made "federal copyright contingent on publication[,] [thereby] providing incentives not primarily for creation," but for dissemination. Perlmutter, *supra*, at 324, n. 5. Our decisions correspondingly recognize that "copyright supplies the economic incentive to create *and disseminate* ideas." *Harper & Row, Publishers, Inc.* v. *Nation Enterprises*, 471 U. S. 539, 558 (1985) (emphasis added). See also *Eldred*, 537 U. S., at 206.[27]

Considered against this backdrop, §514 falls comfortably within Congress' authority under the Copyright Clause. Congress rationally could have concluded that adherence to Berne "promotes the diffusion of knowledge," Brief for Petitioners 4. A well-functioning international copyright system would likely encourage the dissemination of existing and future works. See URAA Joint Hearing 189 (statement of Professor Perlmutter). Full compliance with Berne, Congress had reason to believe, would expand the foreign markets available to U. S. authors and invigorate protection against piracy of U. S. works abroad, S. Rep. No. 103–412, pp. 224, 225 (1994); URAA Joint Hearing 291 (statement of Berman, RIAA); *id.*, at 244, 247 (statement of Smith, IIPA), thereby benefitting copyright-intensive industries stateside and inducing greater investment in the creative process.

The provision of incentives for the creation of new works is surely an essential means to advance the spread of knowledge and learning. We hold, however, that it is not the sole means Congress may use "[t]o promote the Progress of Science." See Perlmutter, *supra*, at 332 (United States would "lose all flexibility" were the provision of incentives to create the exclusive way to promote the progress of science).[28] Congress determined that exemplary adherence to Berne would serve the objectives of the Copyright Clause. We have no warrant to reject the rational judgment Congress made.

III

A

We next explain why the First Amendment does not inhibit the restoration authorized by §514. To do so, we first recapitulate the relevant part of our pathmarking decision in *Eldred.* The petitioners in *Eldred*, like those here, argued that Congress had violated not only the "limited Times" prescription of the Copyright Clause. In addition, and independently, the *Eldred* petitioners charged, Congress had offended the First Amendment's freedom of expression guarantee. The CTEA's 20-year enlargement of a copyright's duration, we held in *Eldred*, offended neither provision.

Concerning the First Amendment, we recognized that some restriction on expression is the inherent and intended effect of every grant of copyright. Noting that the "Copyright Clause and the First Amendment were adopted close in time," 537 U. S., at 219, we observed that the Framers regarded copyright protection not simply as a limit on the manner in which expressive works may be used. They also saw copyright as an "engine of free expression[:] By establishing a marketable right to the use of one's expression, copyright supplies the economic incentive to create and disseminate ideas." *Ibid.* (quoting *Harper & Row*, 471 U. S., at 558 (internal quotation marks omitted)); see *id.*, at 546 ("rights conferred by copyright are designed to assure contributors to the store of knowledge a fair return for their labors").

We then described the "traditional contours" of copyright protection, *i.e.*, the "idea/expression dichotomy" and the "fair use" defense.[29] Both are recognized in our jurisprudence as "built-in First Amendment accommodations." *Eldred*, 537 U. S., at 219; see *Harper & Row*, 471 U. S., at 560 (First Amendment protections are "embodied in the Copyright Act's distinction between copyrightable expression and uncopyrightable facts and ideas," and in the "latitude for scholarship and comment" safeguarded by the fair use defense).

The idea/expression dichotomy is codified at 17 U. S. C. §102(b): "In no case does copyright protec[t] … any idea, procedure, process, system, method of operation, concept, principle, or discovery … described, explained, illustrated, or embodied in [the copyrighted] work." "Due to this [idea/expression] distinction, every idea, theory, and fact in a copyrighted work becomes instantly available for public exploitation at the moment of publication"; the author's expression alone gains copyright protection. *Eldred*, 537 U. S., at 219; see *Harper & Row*, 471 U. S., at 556 ("idea/expression dichotomy strike[s] a definitional balance between the First Amendment and the

Copyright Act by permitting free communication of facts while still protecting an author's expression" (internal quotation marks omitted)).

The second "traditional contour," the fair use defense, is codified at 17 U. S. C. §107: "[T]he fair use of a copyrighted work, including such use by reproduction in copies … , for purposes such as criticism, comment, news reporting, teaching (including multiple copies for classroom use), scholarship, or research, is not an infringement of copyright." This limitation on exclusivity "allows the public to use not only facts and ideas contained in a copyrighted work, but also [the author's] expression itself in certain circumstances." *Eldred*, 537 U. S., at 219; see *id.,* at 220 ("fair use defense affords considerable latitude for scholarship and comment, ... even for parody" (internal quotation marks omitted)).

Given the "speech-protective purposes and safeguards" embraced by copyright law, see *id.,* at 219, we concluded in *Eldred* that there was no call for the heightened review petitioners sought in that case.[30] We reach the same conclusion here.[31] Section 514 leaves undisturbed the "idea/expression" distinction and the "fair use" defense. Moreover, Congress adopted measures to ease the transition from a national scheme to an international copyright regime: It deferred the date from which enforcement runs, and it cushioned the impact of restoration on "reliance parties" who exploited foreign works denied protection before §514 took effect. See *supra,* at 10–11 (describing 17 U. S. C. §104A(c), (d), and (h)). See also *Eldred*, 537 U. S., at 220 (describing supplemental allowances and exemptions available to certain users to mitigate the CTEA's impact).

B

Petitioners attempt to distinguish their challenge from the one turned away in *Eldred.* First Amendment interests of a higher order are at stake here, petitioners say, because they—unlike their counterparts in *Eldred*— enjoyed "vested rights" in works that had already entered the public domain. The limited rights they retain under copyright law's "built-in safeguards" are, in their view, no substitute for the unlimited use they enjoyed before §514's enactment. Nor, petitioners urge, does §514's "unprecedented" foray into the public domain possess the historical pedigree that supported the term extension at issue in *Eldred.* Brief for Petitioners 42–43.

However spun, these contentions depend on an argument we considered and rejected above, namely, that the Constitution renders the public domain largely untouchable by Congress. Petitioners here attempt to achieve under the banner of the First Amendment what they could not win under the Copyright

Clause: On their view of the Copyright Clause, the public domain is inviolable; as they read the First Amendment, the public domain is policed through heightened judicial scrutiny of Congress' means and ends. As we have already shown, see *supra,* at 13–19, the text of the Copyright Clause and the historical record scarcely establish that "once a work enters the public domain," Congress cannot permit anyone—"not even the creator—[to] copyright it," 501 F. 3d, at 1184. And nothing in the historical record, congressional practice, or our own jurisprudence warrants exceptional First Amendment solicitude for copyrighted works that were once in the public domain.[32] Neither this challenge nor that raised in *Eldred*, we stress, allege Congress transgressed a generally applicable First Amendment prohibition; we are not faced, for example, with copyright protection that hinges on the author's viewpoint.

The Tenth Circuit's initial opinion determined that petitioners marshaled a stronger First Amendment challenge than did their predecessors in *Eldred*, who never "possessed unfettered access to any of the works at issue." 501 F. 3d, at 1193. See also *id.,* at 1194 ("[O]nce the works at issue became free for anyone to copy, [petitioners] had vested First Amendment interests in the expressions, [thus] §514's interference with [petitioners'] rights is subject to First Amendment scrutiny."). As petitioners put it in this Court, Congress impermissibly revoked their right to exploit foreign works that "belonged to them" once the works were in the public domain. Brief for Petitioners 44–45.

To copyright lawyers, the "vested rights" formulation might sound exactly backwards: Rights typically vest at the *outset* of copyright protection, in an author or rightholder. See, *e.g.*, 17 U. S. C. §201(a) ("Copyright in a work protected … vests initially in the author …."). Once the term of protection ends, the works do not revest in any rightholder. Instead, the works simply lapse into the public domain. See, *e.g.*, Berne, Art. 18(1), 828 U. N. T. S., at 251 ("This Convention shall apply to all works which … have not yet fallen into the public domain ..."). Anyone has free access to the public domain, but no one, after the copyright term has expired, acquires ownership rights in the once-protected works.

Congress recurrently adjusts copyright law to protect categories of works once outside the law's compass. For example, Congress broke new ground when it extended copyright protection to foreign works in 1891, Act of Mar. 3, §13, 26 Stat. 1110; to dramatic works in 1856, Act of Aug. 18, 11 Stat. 138; to photographs and photographic negatives in 1865, Act of Mar. 3, §1, 13 Stat. 540; to motion pictures in 1912, Act of Aug. 24, 37 Stat. 488; to fixed sound recordings in 1972, Act of Oct. 15, 1971, 85 Stat. 391; and to architectural works in 1990, Architectural Works Copyright Protection Act, 104 Stat. 5133. And on several occasions, as recounted above, Congress protected works previously in the public domain, hence freely usable by the public. See *supra,* at 15–19. If Congress could grant protection to these works without hazarding heightened First Amendment scrutiny, then what free speech principle disarms it from protecting works prematurely cast into the public domain for reasons antithetical to the Berne Convention?[33]

Section 514, we add, does not impose a blanket prohibition on public access. Petitioners protest that fair use and the idea/expression dichotomy "are plainly inadequate to protect the speech and expression rights that Section 514 took from petitioners, or ... the public"—that is, "the unrestricted right to perform, copy, teach and distribute the *entire* work, for any reason." Brief for Petitioners 46– 47. "Playing a few bars of a Shostakovich symphony," petitioners observe, "is no substitute for performing the entire work." *Id.*, at 47.[34]

But Congress has not put petitioners in this bind. The question here, as in *Eldred*, is whether would-be users must pay for their desired use of the author's expression, or else limit their exploitation to "fair use" of that work. Prokofiev's Peter and the Wolf could once be performed free of charge; after §514 the right to perform it must be obtained in the marketplace. This is the same marketplace, of course, that exists for the music of Prokofiev's U. S. contemporaries: works of Copland and Bernstein, for example, that enjoy copyright protection, but nevertheless appear regularly in the programs of U. S. concertgoers.

Before we joined Berne, domestic works and some foreign works were protected under U. S. statutes and bilateral international agreements, while other foreign works were available at an artificially low (because royalty-free) cost. By fully implementing Berne, Congress ensured that most works, whether foreign or domestic, would be governed by the same legal regime. The phenomenon to which Congress responded is not new: Distortions of the same order occurred with greater frequency—and to the detriment of both foreign and domestic authors—when, before 1891, foreign works were excluded entirely from U. S. copyright protection. See Kampelman, The United States and International Copyright, 41 Am. J. Int'l L. 406, 413 (1947) ("American readers were less inclined to read the novels of Cooper or Hawthorne for a dollar when they could buy a novel of Scott or Dickens for a quarter."). Section 514 continued the trend toward a harmonized copyright regime by placing foreign works in the position they would have occupied if the current regime had been in effect when those works were created and first published. Authors once deprived of protection are spared the continuing effects of that initial deprivation; §514 gives them nothing more than the benefit of their labors during whatever time remains before the normal copyright term expires.[35]

Unlike petitioners, the dissent makes much of the so-called "orphan works" problem. See *post*, at 11–14, 23–24. We readily acknowledge the difficulties would-be users of copyrightable materials may face in identifying or locating copyright owners. See generally U. S. Copyright Office, Report on Orphan Works 21–40 (2006). But as the dissent concedes, see *post*, at 13, this difficulty is hardly peculiar to works restored under §514. It similarly afflicts, for instance, U. S. libraries that attempt to catalogue U. S. books. See *post,* at 12. See also Brief for American Library Association et al. as *Amici Curiae* 22 (Section 514 "exacerbated," but did not create, the problem of orphan works); U. S. Copyright Office, *supra,* at 41–44 (tracing orphan-works problem to Congress' elimination of formalities, commencing with the 1976 Copyright Act).[36]

Nor is this a matter appropriate for judicial, as opposed to legislative, resolution. Cf. *Authors Guild* v. *Google, Inc.*, 770 F. Supp. 2d 666, 677–678 (SDNY 2011) (rejecting proposed "Google Books" class settlement because, *inter alia*, "the establishment of a mechanism for exploiting unclaimed books is a matter more suited for Congress than this Court" (citing *Eldred*, 537 U. S., at 212)). Indeed, the host of policy and logistical questions identified by the dissent speak for themselves. *Post*, at 12. Despite "longstanding efforts," see *Authors Guild*, 770 F. Supp. 2d, at 678 (quoting statement of Marybeth Peters), Congress has not yet passed ameliorative orphan-works legislation of the sort enacted by other Berne members, see, *e.g.*, Canada Copyright Act, R. S. C., 1985, c. C–42, §77 (authorizing Copyright Board to license use of orphan works by persons unable, after making reasonable efforts, to locate the copyright owner). Heretofore, no one has suggested that the orphan-works issue should be addressed through our implementation of Berne, rather than through overarching legislation of the sort proposed in Congress and cited by the dissent. See *post,* at 23–24; U. S. Copyright Office, Legal Issues in Mass Digitization 25–29 (2011) (discussing recent legislative efforts). Our unstinting adherence to Berne may add impetus to calls for the enactment of such legislation. But resistance to Berne's prescriptions surely is not a necessary or proper response to the pervasive question, what should Congress do about orphan works.

IV

Congress determined that U. S. interests were best served by our full participation in the dominant system of international copyright protection. Those interests include ensuring exemplary compliance with our international obligations, securing greater protection for U. S. authors abroad, and remedying unequal treatment of foreign authors. The judgment §514 expresses lies well within the ken of the political branches. It is our obligation, of course, to determine whether the action Congress took, wise or not, encounters any constitutional shoal. For the reasons stated, we are satisfied it does not. The judgment of the Court of Appeals for the Tenth Circuit is therefore

Affirmed.

JUSTICE KAGAN took no part in the consideration or decision of this case.

APPENDIX

Title 17 U. S. C. §104A provides:

"(a) AUTOMATIC PROTECTION AND TERM.—

"(1) TERM.—

"(A) Copyright subsists, in accordance with this section, in restored works, and vests automatically on the date of restoration.

"(B) Any work in which copyright is restored under this section shall subsist for the remainder of the term of copyright that the work would have otherwise been granted in the United States if the work never entered the public domain in the United States.

"(2) EXCEPTION.—Any work in which the copyright was ever owned or administered by the Alien Property Custodian and in which the restored copyright would be owned by a government or instrumentality thereof, is not a restored work.

"(b) OWNERSHIP OF RESTORED COPYRIGHT.—A restored work vests initially in the author or initial rightholder of the work as determined by the law of the source country of the work.

"(c) FILING OF NOTICE OF INTENT TO ENFORCE RESTORED COPYRIGHT AGAINST RELIANCE PARTIES.—On or after the date of restoration, any person who owns a copyright in a restored work or an exclusive right therein may file with the Copyright Office a notice of intent to enforce that person's copyright or exclusive right or may serve such a notice directly on a reliance party. Acceptance of a notice by the Copyright Office is effective as to any reliance parties but shall not create a presumption of the validity of any of the facts stated therein. Service on a reliance party is effective as to that reliance party and any other reliance parties with actual knowledge of such service and of the contents of that notice.

"(d) REMEDIES FOR INFRINGEMENT OF RESTORED COPYRIGHTS.—

"(1) ENFORCEMENT OF COPYRIGHT IN RESTORED WORKS IN THE ABSENCE OF A RELIANCE PARTY.—As against any party who is not a reliance party, the remedies provided in chapter 5 of this title shall be available on or after the date of restoration of a restored copyright with respect to an act of infringement of the restored copyright that is commenced on or after the date of restoration.

"(2) ENFORCEMENT OF COPYRIGHT IN RESTORED WORKS AS AGAINST RELIANCE PARTIES.—As against a reliance party, except to the extent provided in paragraphs (3) and (4), the remedies provided in chapter 5 of this title shall be available, with respect to an act of infringement of a restored copyright, on or after the date of restoration of the restored copyright if the requirements of either of the following subparagraphs are met:

"(A)(i) The owner of the restored copyright (or such owner's agent) or the owner of an exclusive right therein (or such owner's agent) files with the Copyright Office, during the 24-month period beginning on the date of restoration, a notice of intent to enforce the restored copyright; and

"(ii)(I) the act of infringement commenced after the end of the 12-month period beginning on the date of publication of the notice in the Federal Register;

"(II) the act of infringement commenced before the end of the 12-month period described in subclause (I) and continued after the end of that 12-month period, in which case remedies shall be available only for infringement occurring after the end of that 12-month period; or copies or phonorecords of a work in which copyright has been restored under this section are made after publication of the notice of intent in the Federal Register.

"(B)(i) The owner of the restored copyright (or such owner's agent) or the owner of an exclusive right therein (or such owner's agent) serves upon a reliance party a notice of intent to enforce a restored copyright; and "(ii)(I) the act of infringement commenced after the end of the 12-month period beginning on the date the notice of intent is received;

"(II) the act of infringement commenced before the end of the 12-month period described in subclause (I) and continued after the end of that 12-month period, in which case remedies shall be available only for the infringement occurring after the end of that 12-month period; or

"(III) copies or phonorecords of a work in which copyright has been restored under this section are made after receipt of the notice of intent.

"In the event that notice is provided under both subparagraphs (A) and (B), the 12-month period referred to in such subparagraphs shall run from the earlier of publication or service of notice.

"(3) EXISTING DERIVATIVE WORKS.—(A) In the case of a derivative work that is based upon a restored work and is created—

"(i) before the date of the enactment of the Uruguay Round Agreements Act, if the source country of the restored work is an eligible country on such date, or

"(ii) before the date on which the source country of the restored work becomes an eligible country, if that country is not an eligible country on such date of enactment, "a reliance party may continue to exploit that derivative work for the duration of the restored copyright if the reliance party pays to the owner of the restored copyright reasonable compensation for conduct which would be subject to a remedy for infringement but for the provisions of this paragraph.

"(B) In the absence of an agreement between the parties, the amount of such compensation shall be determined by an action in United States district court, and shall reflect any harm to the actual or potential market for or value of the restored work from the reliance party's continued exploitation of the work, as well as compensation for the relative contributions of expression of the author of the restored work and the reliance party to the derivative work.

"(4) COMMENCEMENT OF INFRINGEMENT FOR RELIANCE PARTIES.—For purposes of section 412, in the case of reliance parties, infringement shall be deemed to have commenced before registration when acts which would have constituted infringement had the restored work been subject to copyright were commenced before the date of restoration.

"(e) NOTICES OF INTENT TO ENFORCE A RESTORED COPYRIGHT.—

"(1) NOTICES OF INTENT FILED WITH THE COPYRIGHT OFFICE.—(A)(i) A notice of intent filed with the Copyright Office to enforce a restored copyright shall be signed by the owner of the restored copyright or the owner of an exclusive right therein, who files the notice under subsection (d)(2)(A)(i) (hereafter in this paragraph referred to as the "owner"), or by the owner's agent, shall identify the title of the restored work, and shall include an English translation of the title and any other alternative titles known to the owner by which the restored work may be identified, and an address and telephone number at which the owner may be contacted. If the notice is signed by an agent, the agency relationship must have been constituted in a writing signed by the owner before the filing of the notice. The Copyright Office may specifically require in regulations other information to be included in the notice, but failure to provide such other information shall not invalidate the notice or be a basis for refusal to list the restored work in the Federal Register.

"(ii) If a work in which copyright is restored has no formal title, it shall be described in the notice of intent in detail sufficient to identify it.

"(iii) Minor errors or omissions may be corrected by further notice at any time after the notice of intent is filed. Notices of corrections for such minor errors or omissions shall be accepted after the period established in subsection (d)(2)(A)(i). Notices shall be published in the Federal Register pursuant to subparagraph (B).

"(B)(i) The Register of Copyrights shall publish in the Federal Register, commencing not later than 4 months after the date of restoration for a particular nation and every 4 months thereafter for a period of 2 years, lists identifying restored works and the ownership thereof if a notice of intent to enforce a restored copyright has been filed.

"(ii) Not less than 1 list containing all notices of intent to enforce shall be maintained in the Public Information Office of the Copyright Office and shall be available for public inspection and copying during regular business hours pursuant to sections 705 and 708.

"(C) The Register of Copyrights is authorized to fix reasonable fees based on the costs of receipt, processing, recording, and publication of notices of intent to enforce a restored copyright and corrections thereto.

"(D)(i) Not later than 90 days before the date the Agreement on Trade-Related Aspects of Intellectual Property referred to in section 101(d)(15) of the Uruguay Round Agreements Act enters into force with respect to the United States, the Copyright Office shall issue and publish in the Federal Register regulations governing the filing under this subsection of notices of intent to enforce a restored copyright.

"(ii) Such regulations shall permit owners of restored copyrights to file simultaneously for registration of the restored copyright.

"(2) NOTICES OF INTENT SERVED ON A RELIANCE PARTY.— (A) Notices of intent to enforce a restored copyright may be served on a reliance party at any time after the date of restoration of the restored copyright.

"(B) Notices of intent to enforce a restored copyright served on a reliance party shall be signed by the owner or the owner's agent, shall identify the restored work and the work in which the restored work is used, if any, in detail sufficient to identify them, and shall include an English translation of the title, any other alternative titles known to the owner by which the work may be identified, the use or uses to which the owner objects, and an address and telephone number at which the reliance party may contact the owner. If the notice is signed by an agent, the agency relationship must have been constituted in writing and signed by the owner before service of the notice.

"(3) EFFECT OF MATERIAL FALSE STATEMENTS.—Any material false statement knowingly made with respect to any restored copyright identified in any notice of intent shall make void all claims and assertions made with respect to such restored copyright.

"(f) IMMUNITY FROM WARRANTY AND RELATED LIABILITY.—

"(1) IN GENERAL.—Any person who warrants, promises, or guarantees that a work does not violate an exclusive right granted in section 106 shall not be liable for legal, equitable, arbitral, or administrative relief if the warranty, promise, or guarantee is breached by virtue of the restoration of copyright under this section, if such warranty, promise, or guarantee is made before January 1, 1995.

"(2) PERFORMANCES.—No person shall be required to perform any act if such performance is made infringing by virtue of the restoration of copyright under the provisions of this section, if the obligation to perform was undertaken before January 1, 1995.

"(g) PROCLAMATION OF COPYRIGHT RESTORATION.— Whenever the President finds that a particular foreign nation extends, to works by authors who are nationals or domiciliaries of the United States, restored copyright protection on substantially the same basis as provided under this section, the President may by proclamation extend restored protection provided under this section to any work—

"(1) of which one or more of the authors is, on the date of first publication, a national, domiciliary, or sovereign authority of that nation; or

"(2) which was first published in that nation.

"The President may revise, suspend, or revoke any such proclamation or impose any conditions or limitations on protection under such a proclamation.

"(h) DEFINITIONS.—For purposes of this section and section 109(a):

"(1) The term "date of adherence or proclamation" means the earlier of the date on which a foreign nation which, as of the date the WTO Agreement enters into force with respect to the United States, is not a nation adhering to the Berne Convention or a WTO member country, becomes—

"(A) a nation adhering to the Berne Convention;

"(B) a WTO member country;

"(C) a nation adhering to the WIPO Copyright Treaty;

"(D) a nation adhering to the WIPO Performances and Phonograms Treaty; or

"(E) subject to a Presidential proclamation under subsection (g).

"(2) The "date of restoration" of a restored copyright is—

"(A) January 1, 1996, if the source country of the restored work is a nation adhering to the Berne Convention or a WTO member country on such date, or

"(B) the date of adherence or proclamation, in the case of any other source country of the restored work.

"(3) The term "eligible country" means a nation, other than the United States, that—

"(A) becomes a WTO member country after the date of the enactment of the Uruguay Round Agreements Act;

"(B) on such date of enactment is, or after such date of enactment becomes, a nation adhering to the Berne Convention;

"(C) adheres to the WIPO Copyright Treaty;

"(D) adheres to the WIPO Performances and Phonograms Treaty; or

"(E) after such date of enactment becomes subject to a proclamation under subsection (g).

"(4) The term "reliance party" means any person who—

"(A) with respect to a particular work, engages in acts, before the source country of that work becomes an eligible country, which would have violated section 106 if the restored work had been subject to copyright protection, and who, after the source country becomes an eligible country, continues to engage in such acts;

"(B) before the source country of a particular work becomes an eligible country, makes or acquires 1 or more copies or phonorecords of that work; or

"(C) as the result of the sale or other disposition of a derivative work covered under subsection (d)(3), or significant assets of a person described in subparagraph (A) or (B), is a successor, assignee, or licensee of that person.

"(5) The term "restored copyright" means copyright in a restored work under this section.

"(6) The term "restored work" means an original work of authorship that—

"(A) is protected under subsection (a);

"(B) is not in the public domain in its source country through expiration of term of protection;

"(C) is in the public domain in the United States due to—

"(i) noncompliance with formalities imposed at any time by United States copyright law, including failure of renewal, lack of proper notice, or failure to comply with any manufacturing requirements;

"(ii) lack of subject matter protection in the case of sound recordings fixed before February 15, 1972; or

"(iii) lack of national eligibility;

"(D) has at least one author or rightholder who was, at the time the work was created, a national or domiciliary of an eligible country, and if published, was first published in an eligible country and not published in the United States during the 30-day period following publication in such eligible country; and

"(E) if the source country for the work is an eligible country solely by virtue of its adherence to the WIPO Performances and Phonograms Treaty, is a sound recording.

"(7) The term "rightholder" means the person—

"(A) who, with respect to a sound recording, first fixes a sound recording with authorization, or

"(B) who has acquired rights from the person described in subparagraph (A) by means of any conveyance or by operation of law.

"(8) The "source country" of a restored work is—

"(A) a nation other than the United States

"(B) in the case of an unpublished work—

"(i) the eligible country in which the author or rightholder is a national or domiciliary, or, if a restored work has more than 1 author or rightholder, of which the majority of foreign authors or rightholders are nationals or domiciliaries; or

"(ii) if the majority of authors or rightholders are not foreign, the nation other than the United States which has the most significant contacts with the work; and

"(C) in the case of a published work—

"(i) the eligible country in which the work is first published, or

"(ii) if the restored work is published on the same day in 2 or more eligible countries, the eligible country which has the most significant contacts with the work."

SUPREME COURT OF THE UNITED STATES

Lawrence Golan, et al., Petitioners V. Eric H. Holder, Jr., Attorney General, et al.

No. 10–545
On Writ of Certiorari to the United States Court of Appeals for the Tenth Circuit
[January 18, 2012]
Justice Breyer, with Whom Justice Alito Joins, Dissenting.

In order "[t]o promote the Progress of Science" (by which term the Founders meant "learning" or "knowledge"), the Constitution's Copyright Clause grants Congress the power to "secur[e] for limited Times to Authors . . . the exclusive Right to their ... Writings." Art. I, §8, cl. 8. This "exclusive Right" allows its holder to charge a fee to those who wish to use a copyrighted work, and the ability to charge that fee encourages the production of new material. In this sense, a copyright is, in Macaulay's words, a "tax on readers for the purpose of giving a bounty to writers"—a bounty designed to encourage new production. As the Court said in *Eldred*, "'[t]he economic philosophy behind the [Copyright] [C]lause ... is the conviction that encouragement of individual effort by personal gain is the best way to advance public welfare through the talents of authors and inventors.'" *Eldred* v. *Ashcroft*, 537 U. S. 186, 212, n. 18 (2003) (quoting *Mazer* v. *Stein*, 347 U. S. 201, 219 (1954)). See T. Macaulay, Speeches on Copyright 25 (E. Miller ed. 1913); E. Walterscheid, The Nature of the Intellectual Property Clause: A Study in Historical Perspective 125–126 (2002) (hereinafter Walterscheid).

The statute before us, however, does not encourage anyone to produce a single new work. By definition, it bestows monetary rewards only on owners of old works—works that have already been created and already are in the American public domain. At the same time, the statute inhibits the dissemination of those works, foreign works published abroad after 1923, of which there are many millions, including films, works of art, innumerable photographs, and, of course, books—books that (in the absence of the statute) would assume their rightful places in computer-accessible databases, spreading knowledge throughout the world. See *infra*, at 10–13. In my view, the Copyright Clause does not authorize Congress to enact this statute. And I consequently dissent.

I

The possibility of eliciting new production is, and always has been, an essential precondition for American copyright protection. The Constitution's words, "exclusive Right," "limited Times," "Progress of Science," viewed through the lens of history underscore the legal significance of what the Court in *Eldred* referred to as the "economic philosophy behind the Copyright Clause." 537 U. S., at 212, n. 18 (brackets omitted). That philosophy understands copyright's grants of limited monopoly privileges to authors as private benefits that are conferred for a public reason—to elicit new creation.

Yet, as the Founders recognized, monopoly is a two-edged sword. On the one hand, it can encourage production of new works. In the absence of copyright protection, anyone might freely copy the products of an author's creative labor, appropriating the benefits without incurring the nonrepeatable costs of creation, thereby deterring authors from exerting themselves in the first place. On the other hand, copyright tends to restrict the dissemination (and use) of works once produced either because the absence of competition translates directly into higher consumer prices or because the need to secure copying permission sometimes imposes administrative costs that make it difficult for potential users of a copyrighted work to find its owner and strike a bargain. See W. Landes & R. Posner, The Economic Structure of Intellectual Property Law 68–70, 213–214 (2003). Consequently, the original British copyright statute, the Constitution's Framers, and our case law all have recognized copyright's resulting and necessary call for balance.

At the time the Framers wrote the Constitution, they were well aware of Britain's 18th-century copyright statute, the Statute of Anne, 8 Anne, ch. 19

(1710), and they were aware of the legal struggles that produced it. That statute sought in part to control, and to limit, preexisting monopolies that had emerged in the book trade as a result of the Crown's having previously granted special privileges to royal favorites. The Crown, for example, had chartered the Stationers' Company, permitting it to regulate and to censor works on the government's behalf. The Stationers had thereby acquired control over the disposition of copies of published works, from which emerged the Stationers' copyright—a right conferred on company members, not authors, that was deemed to exist in perpetuity. See L. Patterson, Copyright in Historical Perspective 1–16, 114–150 (1968) (hereinafter Patterson); Walterscheid 59–65; Gómez-Arostegui, The Untold Story of the First Copyright Suit Under the Statute of Anne in 1710, 25 Berkeley Tech. L. J. 1247, 1250–1256 (2010).

To prevent the continuation of the booksellers' monopoly and to encourage authors to write new books, Parliament enacted the Statute of Anne. It bore the title: "An Act for the Encouragement of Learning, by vesting the Copies of printed Books in the Authors or Purchasers of such Copies, during the Times therein mentioned." And it granted authors (not publishers) and their assignees the "sole Right and Liberty of printing" their works for limited periods of time *in order to encourage them "to compose and write useful Books*." 8 Anne, ch. 19, §1 (emphasis added). As one historian has put it, "[t]he central plank of the … Act was … a cultural *quid pro quo*. To encourage 'learned Men to compose and write useful Books' the state would provide a guaranteed, if temporally limited, right to print and reprint those works." Deazley, The Myth of Copyright at Common Law, 62 Camb. L. J. 106, 108 (2003). At first, in their attempts to minimize their losses, the booksellers argued that authors had a perpetual common-law copyright in their works deriving from their natural rights as creators. But the House of Lords ultimately held in *Donaldson* v. *Beckett*, 1 Eng. Rep. 837 (1774), that the Statute of Anne had transformed any such perpetual common-law copyright into a copyright of a limited term designed to serve the public interest. Patterson 15–16, 153, 158–179; Deazley, *supra*, at 114–126.

Many early colonial copyright statutes, patterned after the Statute of Anne, also stated that copyright's objective was to encourage authors to produce new works and thereby improve learning. See U. S. Copyright Office, Copyright Enactments, Bulletin No. 3, pp. 1, 6, 10, 11, 17, 19 (rev. 1963) (statutes of Connecticut, New Jersey, Pennsylvania, South Carolina, Georgia, and New York); Walterscheid 74–75; Bracha, The Adventures of the Statute of Anne in the Land of Unlimited Possibilities: The Life of a Legal Transplant, 25 Berkeley Tech. L. J. 1427, 1444– 1450 (2010).

At least, that was the predominant view expressed to, or by, the Founders. Patterson 93. Thomas Jefferson, for example, initially expressed great uncertainty as to whether the Constitution should authorize the grant of copyrights and patents at all, writing that "the benefit even of limited monopolies is too doubtful" to warrant anything other than their "suppression." Letter from Thomas Jefferson to James Madison (July 31, 1788), in 13 Papers of Thomas Jefferson 440, 443 (J. Boyd ed. 1956). James Madison also thought that "Monopolies … are justly classed among the greatest nu[i]sances in Government." Letter from James Madison to Thomas Jefferson (Oct. 17, 1788), in 14 *id.,* at 16, 21 (J. Boyd ed. 1958). But he argued that "in certain cases" such as copyright, monopolies should "be granted" ("with caution, and guarded with strictness agst abuse") to serve as "*compensation for a benefit actually gained to the community* … which the owner might otherwise withhold from public use." Monopolies. Perpetuities. Corporations. Ecclesiastical Endowments. in J. Madison, Writings 756 (J. Rakove ed. 1999) (emphasis added). Jefferson eventually came to agree with Madison, supporting a limited conferral of monopoly rights but only "*as an encouragement to men to pursue ideas which may produce utility*." Letter from Thomas Jefferson to Isaac McPherson (Aug. 13, 1813), in 6 Papers of Thomas Jefferson, at 379, 383 (J. Looney ed. 2009) (emphasis added).

This utilitarian view of copyrights and patents, embraced by Jefferson and Madison, stands in contrast to the "natural rights" view underlying much of continental European copyright law—a view that the English booksellers promoted in an effort to limit their losses following the enactment of the Statute of Anne and that in part motivated the enactment of some of the colonial statutes. Patterson 158–179, 183–192. Premised on the idea that an author or inventor has an inherent right to the fruits of his labor, it mythically stems from a legendary 6th-century statement of King Diarmed "'to every cow her calf, and accordingly to every book its copy.' " A. Birrell, Seven Lectures on the Law and History of Copyright in Books 42 (1899). That view, though perhaps reflected in the Court's opinion, *ante,* at 30, runs contrary to the more utilitarian views that influenced the writing of our own Constitution's Copyright Clause. See S. Ricketson, The Berne Convention for the Protection of Literary and Artistic Works: 1886–1986, pp. 5–6 (1987) (The first French copyright laws "placed authors' rights on a more elevated basis than the Act of Anne had done," on the understanding that they were "simply according formal recognition to what was already inherent in the 'very nature of things'"); S. Stewart, International Copyright and Neighbouring Rights 6–7 (2d ed. 1989) (describing the European system of *droit d'auteur*).

This utilitarian understanding of the Copyright Clause has long been reflected in the Court's case law. In *Mazer*, for example, the Court refers to copyright as embodying the view that "*encouragement of individual effort by personal gain* is the best way to advance public welfare through the talents of authors and inventors." 347 U. S., at 219 (emphasis added). In *Twentieth Century Music Corp.* v. *Aiken*, 422 U. S. 151 (1975), the Court says that underlying copyright is the understanding that "*[c]reative work is to be encouraged and rewarded, but private motivation must ultimately serve the cause of promoting broad public availability of literature, music, and the other arts.*" *Id.*, at 156 (emphasis added). And in *Sony Corp. of America* v. *Universal City Studios, Inc.*, 464 U. S. 417 (1984), the Court, speaking of both copyrights and patents, points out that the "monopoly privileges that Congress may authorize are … [not] primarily designed to provide a special private benefit. Rather, the limited grant is a means by which an important public purpose may be achieved. It is intended *to motivate the creative activity of authors ... by the provision of a special reward.*" *Id.,* at 429 (emphasis added); see also, *e.g., Graham* v. *John Deere Co. of Kansas City*, 383 U. S. 1, 6 (1966) (The "constitutional command … '[to] promote the Progress [of Science]' … is the *standard* expressed in the Constitution and it may not be ignored"); *Fox Film Corp.* v. *Doyal*, 286 U. S. 123, 127 (1932) ("The sole interest of the United States … lie[s] in the general benefits derived by the public from the labors of authors").

Congress has expressed similar views in congressional Reports on copyright legislation. Thus, for example, an 1892 House Report states:

> "The object to be attained and the reason for the constitutional grant of power are imbedded in the grant itself. They are 'to promote the progress of science and the useful arts.' … [The Clause says] nothing … about any desire or purpose to secure to the author or inventor his 'natural right to his property.'" H. R. Rep. No. 1494, 52d Cong., 1st Sess., 2.

Similarly, the congressional authors of the landmark 1909 Copyright Act wrote:

> "The Constitution … provides that Congress shall have the power to grant [copyrights] … [n]ot primarily for the benefit of the author, … but because the policy is believed to be for the benefit of the great body of people, *in that it will stimulate writing and invention*, to give some bonus to authors and inventors." H. R. Rep. No. 2222, 60th Cong., 2d Sess., 7 (1909).

And they went on to say:

> "Congress must consider … two questions: First, how much will the legislation stimulate the producer and so benefit the public; and, second, how much will the monopoly granted be detrimental to the public? The granting of such exclusive rights, under the proper terms and conditions, confers a benefit upon the public that outweighs the evils of the temporary monopoly." *Ibid.*

The upshot is that text, history, and precedent demonstrate that the Copyright Clause places great value on the power of copyright to elicit new production. Congress in particular cases may determine that copyright's ability to do so outweighs any concomitant high prices, administrative costs, and restrictions on dissemination. And when it does so, we must respect its judgment. See *Eldred,* 537 U. S., at 222. But does the Clause empower Congress to enact a statute that withdraws works from the public domain, brings about higher prices and costs, and in doing so seriously restricts dissemination, particularly to those who need it for scholarly, educational, or cultural pur- poses—all *without providing any additional incentive* for the production of new material? That is the question before us. And, as I have said, I believe the answer is no. Congress in this statute has exceeded what are, under any plausible reading of the Copyright Clause, its permissible limits.

II

The Act before us says that it "restores" American copyright to a set of works, which, for the most part, did not previously enjoy American copyright protection. These works had fallen into America's public domain, but as of the "restoration" date, they had not yet fallen into the public domain of the foreign country where they originated.

The statute covers works originating almost anywhere outside the United States. See 17 U. S. C. §104A(h)(3) (setting out eligibility criteria); U. S. Copyright Office, Circular No. 38A: International Copyright Relations of the United States (2010). The relevant set of works consists primarily of works originating abroad that did not obtain, or at some point lost, American copyright protection because (1) the author failed to comply with applicable American copyright formalities (such as notice or renewal), or (2) the nation in which they were first published then lacked copyright relations with the

United States, or (3) they are sound recordings fixed before February 15, 1972. §104A(h)(6)(C). A work must also satisfy other technical requirements: It must have had a rightholder who was a national or resident of an eligible country on the day it was created; and it cannot have been published in the United States within 30 days of its first publication.

§104A(h)(6)(D). The Act grants these works a copyright that expires at the time it would have expired had the author obtained a full American copyright term starting from the date on which the work was first published (in the foreign country). §104A(a)(1)(B).

The Act mainly applies to works first published abroad between 1923 and 1989. It does not apply significantly to earlier works because any work published before 1921 would have fallen into the public domain before 1977 had it received a full American copyright term, while works published between 1921 and 1923 obtained a "restored" copyright that expired before the 1998 Sonny Bono Copyright Term Extension Act, and so could have lasted two years at most. See Tit. I, §101, 90 Stat. 2574 (extending the copyright term of works still under copyright in 1977 to 75 years); 17 U. S. C. §304(b) (extending the copyright term of works still under copyright in 1998 to 95 years). It has less impact on more recent works because in 1989 the United States became a Berne member, abolished the copyright notice requirement, and thenceforth provided prospective copyright protection throughout the Berne Union. See R. Schechter & J. Thomas, Intellectual Property: The Law of Copyrights, Patents and Trademarks 75– 77 (2003); §7, 102 Stat. 2857–2858 (codified as amended at 17 U. S. C. §§401–406).

Despite these temporal limitations, the Act covers vast numbers of works. The first category includes works published in countries that had copyright relations with the United States during this time period, such as most of Western Europe and Latin America, Australia, and Japan, see Circular No. 38A, *supra,* at 2–10, whose authors did not satisfy American copyright formalities, perhaps because the author, who may not have sought an American copyright, published the book abroad without proper American notice, or perhaps because the author obtained a valid American copyright but failed to renew it.

The second category (works that entered the public domain due to a lack of copyright relations) includes, among others, all works published in Russia and other countries of the former Soviet Union before May 1973 (when the U. S. S. R. joined the Universal Copyright Convention (UCC)), all works published in the People's Republic of China before March 1992 (when bilateral copyright relations between the People's Republic and the United

States were first established), all South Korean works published before October 1987 (when South Korea joined the UCC), and all Egyptian and Turkish works published before March 1989 (when the United States joined Berne). See *id.*, at 2–10, and 11, nn. 2, 5, 6.

The third category covers all sound recordings from eligible foreign countries published after February 15, 1972. The practical significance of federal copyright restoration to this category of works is less clear, since these works received, and continued to receive, copyright protection under state law. See 17 U. S. C. §301(c).

Apparently there are no precise figures about the number of works the Act affects, but in 1996 the then-Register of Copyrights, Marybeth Peters, thought that they "probably number in the millions." The Year in Review: Accomplishments and Objectives of the U. S. Copyright Office, 7 Ford. Intellectual Property Media & Entertainment L. J. 25, 31 (1996).

A

The provision before us takes works from the public domain, at least as of January 1, 1996. See §104A(h)(2)(A) (setting "restoration" dates). It then restricts the dissemination of those works in two ways.

First, "restored copyright" holders can now charge fees for works that consumers previously used for free. The price of a score of Shostakovich's Preludes and Fugues Op. 87, for example, has risen by a multiple of seven. Brief for Conductors Guild et al. as *Amici Curiae* 11. And, as the Court recognizes, an orchestra that once could perform "Peter and the Wolf … free of charge" will now have to buy the "right to perform it … in the marketplace." *Ante,* at 29. But for the case of certain "derivative" works, §104A(d)(3), the "restored copyright" holder, like other copyright holders, can charge what the market will bear. If a school orchestra or other nonprofit organization cannot afford the new charges, so be it. They will have to do without—aggravating the already serious problem of cultural education in the United States. See Brief for Conductors Guild et al. as *Amici Curiae* 4–5, 7–8 (describing the inability of many orchestras to pay for the rental of sheet music covered by "restored copyright[s]").

Second, and at least as important, the statute creates administrative costs, such as the costs of determining whether a work is the subject of a "restored copyright," searching for a "restored copyright" holder, and negotiating a fee. Congress has tried to ease the administrative burden of contacting copyright holders and negotiating prices for those whom the statute calls "reliance part[ies]," namely those who previously had used such works when they were freely available in the public domain. §104A(h)(4). But Congress has done nothing to ease the administrative burden of securing permission from copyright owners that is placed upon those who want to use a work that they did not previously use, and this is a particular problem when it comes to "orphan works"—older and more obscure works with minimal commercial value that have copyright owners who are difficult or impossible to track down. Unusually high administrative costs threaten to limit severely the distribution and use of those works— works which, despite their characteristic lack of economic value, can prove culturally invaluable.

There are millions of such works. For example, according to European Union figures, there are 13 million orphan books in the European Union (13% of the total number of books in-copyright there), 225,000 orphan films in European film archives, and 17 million orphan photographs in United Kingdom museums. A. Vuopala, Assessment of the Orphan works issue and Costs for Rights Clearance 19, 25 (2010), online at http://ec.europa.eu/information_society/activities/digital_libraries/doc/reports_orphan/anna_report.pdf (all Internet materials as visited Jan. 13, 2012, and available in Clerk of Court's case file). How is a university, a film collector, a musician, a database compiler, or a scholar now to obtain permission to use any such lesser known foreign work previously in the American public domain? Consider the questions that any such individual, group, or institution usually must answer: Is the work eligible for restoration under the statute? If so, who now holds the copyright—the author? an heir? a publisher? an association? a long-lost cousin? Whom must we contact? What is the address? Suppose no one answers? How do we conduct a negotiation?

To find answers to these, and similar questions, costs money. The cost to the University of Michigan and the Institute of Museum and Library Services, for example, to determine the copyright status of books contained in the HathiTrust Digital Library that were published in the United States from 1923 to 1963 will exceed $1 million. Brief for American Library Assn. et al. as *Amici Curiae* 15.

It is consequently not surprising to learn that the Los Angeles Public Library has been unable to make its collection of Mexican folk music publicly available because of problems locating copyright owners, that a Jewish cultural organization has abandoned similar efforts to make available Jewish cultural music and other materials, or that film preservers, museums, universities, scholars, database compilers, and others report that the administrative costs associated with trying to locate foreign copyright owners have forced them to curtail their cultural, scholarly, or other work-preserving efforts. See, *e.g.,* Comments of the Library Copyright Alliance in Response to the U. S. Copyright Office's Inquiry on Orphan Works 5 (Mar. 25, 2005), online at http://www.arl.org/bm~doc/lcacomment0305.pdf; Comments of Creative Commons and Save The Music in Response to the U. S. Copyright Office's Inquiry on Orphan Works (Mar. 25, 2005), online at http://www.copyright.gov/orphan/comments/OW0643-STMCreativeCommons.pdf; General Agreement on Tariffs and Trade (GATT): Intellectual Property Provisions, Joint Hearing before the Subcommittee on Intellectual Property and Judicial Administration of the House Committee on the Judiciary and the Subcommittee on Patents, Copyrights and Trademarks of the Senate Committee on the Judiciary, 103d Cong., 2d Sess., 131, 273 (1994) (hereinafter Joint Hearing) (statement of Larry Urbanski, Chairman of the Fairness in Copyright Coalition and President of Moviecraft, Inc.); Brief for American Library Assn. et al. as *Amici Curiae* 6–23; Brief for Creative Commons Corp. as *Amicus Curiae* 7–8; Brief for Project Petrucci, LLC, as *Amicus Curiae* 10–11.

These high administrative costs can prove counterproductive in another way. They will tempt some potential users to "steal" or "pirate" works rather than do without. And piracy often begets piracy, breeding the destructive habit of taking copyrighted works without paying for them, even where payment is possible. Such habits ignore the critical role copyright plays in the creation of new works, while reflecting a false belief that new creation appears by magic without thought or hope of compensation.

B

I recognize that ordinary copyright protection also comes accompanied with dissemination-restricting royalty charges and administrative costs. But here the restrictions work special harm. For one thing, the foreign location of restored works means higher than ordinary administrative costs. For another, the statute's technical requirements make it very difficult to establish whether a work has had its copyright restored by the statute. Gard, In the Trenches with §104A: An Evaluation of the Parties' Arguments in *Golan v. Holder* as It Heads to the Supreme Court, 64 Vand. L. Rev. En Banc 199, 216–220 (2011) (describing difficulties encountered in compiling the information necessary to create an online tool to determine whether the statute applies in any given case).

Worst of all, "restored copyright" protection removes material from the public domain. In doing so, it reverses the payment expectations of those who used, or intended to use, works that they thought belonged to them. Were

Congress to act similarly with respect to well-established property rights, the problem would be obvious. This statute analogously restricts, and thereby diminishes, Americans' preexisting freedom to use formerly public domain material in their expressive activities.

Thus, while the majority correctly observes that the dissemination-restricting harms of copyright normally present problems appropriate for legislation to resolve, *ante,* at 31–32, the question is whether the Copyright Clause permits Congress seriously to exacerbate such a problem by taking works out of the public domain without a countervailing benefit. This question *is* appropriate for judicial resolution. Indeed, unlike *Eldred* where the Court had to decide a complicated line-drawing question—when is a copyright term too long?—here an easily administrable standard is available—a standard that would require works that have already fallen into the public domain to stay there.

The several, just mentioned features of the present statute are important, for they distinguish it from other copyright laws. By removing material from the public domain, the statute, in literal terms, "abridges" a preexisting freedom to speak. In practical terms, members of the public might well have decided what to say, as well as when and how to say it, in part by reviewing with a view to repeating, expression that they reasonably believed was, or would be, freely available. Given these speech implications, it is not surprising that Congress has long sought to protect public domain material when revising the copyright laws. See *infra*, at 19 (listing instances). And this Court has assumed the particular importance of public domain material in roughly analogous circumstances. See *Graham*, 383 U. S., at 6 ("Congress may not authorize the issuance of patents whose effects are to remove existent knowledge from the public domain"); *Kewanee Oil Co.* v. *Bicron Corp.*, 416 U. S. 470, 484 (1974) (trade secret protection is not incompatible with "policy that matter once in the public domain must remain in the public domain"); *Cox Broadcasting Corp.* v. *Cohn*, 420 U. S. 469, 496 (1975) (First Amendment prohibits sanctioning press for publishing material disclosed in public court documents); see also *Dastar Corp.* v. *Twentieth Century Fox Film Corp.*, 539 U. S. 23, 33 (2003) ("The right to copy ... once a copyright has expired ... passes to the public" (internal quotation marks omitted)).

Moreover, whereas forward-looking copyright laws tend to benefit those whose identities are not yet known (the writer who has not yet written a book, the musician who has not yet composed a song), when a copyright law is primarily backward looking the risk is greater that Congress is trying to help known beneficiaries at the expense of badly organized unknown users who find it difficult to argue and present their case to Congress. In *Eldred*, I thought this problem was severe. See generally 537 U. S., at 243–266 (dissenting opinion). And in light of the fact that Congress, with one minor exception, heard testimony only from the representatives of existing copyright holders, who hoped that passage of the statute would enable them to benefit from reciprocal treatment of American authors abroad, *infra*, at 21, I cannot say that even here the problem, while much diminished, was nonexistent.

I agree with the majority that, in doing so, this statute does not discriminate among speakers based on their viewpoints or subject matter. *Ante,* at 27. But such considerations do not exhaust potential First Amendment problems. Cf. *Sorrell* v. *IMS Health Inc.*, 564 U. S. ___, ___ (2011) (slip op., at 8) (finding First Amendment problem in statute that prohibits drug manufacturers from using publicly available prescriber-identifying information in their marketing efforts in part because it "disfavor[ed] specific speakers"); *Turner Broadcasting System, Inc.* v. *FCC*, 512 U. S. 622, 659 (1994) ("Regulations that discriminate among media, or among different speakers within a single medium, often present serious First Amendment concerns").

Taken together, these speech-related harms (*e.g.,* restricting use of previously available material; reversing payment expectations; rewarding rent-seekers at the public's expense) at least show the presence of a First Amendment interest. And that is enough. For present purposes, I need not decide whether the harms to that interest show a violation of the First Amendment. I need only point to the importance of interpreting the Constitution as a single document—a document that we should not read as setting the Copyright Clause and the First Amendment at cross-purposes. Nor need I advocate the application here of strict or specially heightened review. I need only find that the First Amendment interest is important enough to require courts to scrutinize with some care the reasons claimed to justify the Act in order to determine whether they constitute reasonable copyright-related justifications for the serious harms, including speech-related harms, which the Act seems likely to impose.

C

1

This statute does not serve copyright's traditional public ends, namely the creation of monetary awards that "motivate the creative activity of authors," *Sony*, 464 U. S., at 429, "encourag[e] individual effort," *Mazer,* 347 U. S., at 219, and thereby "serve the cause of promoting broad public availability of literature, music, and the other arts." *Twentieth Century Music*, 422 U. S., at 156. The statute grants its "restored copyright[s]" *only* to works *already produced.* It provides no monetary incentive to produce anything new. Unlike other American copyright statutes from the time of the Founders onwards, including the statute at issue in *Eldred*, it lacks any significant copyright-related *quid pro quo.*

The majority seeks to avoid this awkward fact by referring to past congressional practice that mostly suggests that Congress may provide new or increased protection *both* to newly created *and* to previously created, works. *Ante,* at 16, 18; Act of May 31, 1790, §1, 1 Stat. 124 (conferring its new federal copyright on new works as well as old); Act of July 3, 1832, §3, 4 Stat. 559 (authorizing new patents for past and future inventors who inadvertently failed to comply with applicable statutory formalities); *McClurg* v. *Kingsland*, 1 How. 202 (1843) (applying an act deeming a past or future inventor's patent valid despite it being briefly used by, for example, the inventor's employer). I do not dispute that copyright power. Insofar as such a statute does the former, *i.e.,* extends protection to newly created material, it embodies copyright's traditional justification—eliciting new production. And I do not doubt that Congress may then also include existing works within the scope of, say, increased protection for equitable and administrative reasons. See *Eldred*, 537 U. S. at 204, 214–215 (describing equitable reasons for applying newly extended copyright terms to future and existing copyrights alike). The statute before us, however, does not directly elicit any new production. Compare *id.,* at 204–208; (majority opinion) (noting that statute's extended term would apply to newly created material, and finding that the determination of the likelihood of its eliciting new production in practice was a matter for Congress to determine), with *id.*, at 243–267 (BREYER, J., dissenting) (expressing the view that there is little likelihood, in practice, that the statute would elicit new material). See also Walterscheid 219 (the 1790 Congress likely thought it was substituting federal protection for preexisting state common-law protections); Maher, Copyright Term, Retrospective Extension, and the Copyright Law of 1790 in Historical Context, 49 J. Copyright Soc. USA 1021, 1023–1024, and n. 8 (2002) (numerical estimate suggesting that 1790 Act removed only a small number of books from public domain).

The other statutes to which the majority refers are private bills, statutes retroactively granting protection in wartime, or the like. *Ante,* at 16–19; Act of Feb. 19, 1849, ch. 57, 9 Stat. 763 (Levi Corson); Act of June 23, 1874, ch. 534, 18 Stat., pt. 3, p. 618 (Tod Helmuth); Act of Feb. 17, 1898, ch. 29, 30 Stat. 1396 (Judson Jones); Act of Dec. 18, 1919, ch. 11, 41 Stat. 368; Act of

Sept. 25, 1941, ch. 421, 55 Stat. 732; see also *Evans* v. *Jordan*, 9 Cranch 199 (1815) (upholding a private bill restoring patent protection to a flour mill). But special circumstances, like wars, hurricanes, earthquakes, and other disasters, prevent the realization in practice of a reasonable expectation of securing or maintaining a preexisting right. Private bills are designed to provide special exceptions for comparable equitable reasons. See also Act of Mar. 3, 1893, ch. 215, 27 Stat. 743 (similar, as far as I can tell). To find in these laws an important analogy to the present law, which for the most part covers works that the author did not expect to protect in America (and often did not particularly want to protect), seems somewhat farfetched.

In fact, Congressional practice shows the contrary. It consists of a virtually unbroken string of legislation preventing the withdrawal of works from the public domain. See, *e.g.,* Berne Convention Implementation Act of 1988, §12, 102 Stat. 2860 (the Act "does not provide copyright protection for any work that is in the public domain in the United States"); Copyright Act of 1976, Tit. I, §101, 90 Stat. 2573 (declining to extend copyright protection to any work that is in the public domain prior to the Act taking effect); Copyright Act of 1909, §7, 35 Stat. 1077 ("[N]o copyright shall subsist in the original text of any work which is in the public domain, or in any work which was published in this country or any foreign country prior to the going into effect of this Act and has not been already copyrighted in the United States"); Act to Amend the Several Acts Respecting Copy Rights §16, 4 Stat. 439 (the Act "shall not extend to any copyright heretofore secured, the term of which has already expired"); see also H. R. Rep. No. 1742, 87th Cong., 2d Sess., 3 (1962) (expressing concern that because "it is not possible to revive expired terms of copyright, it seems to the committee to be desirable to suspend further expiration of copyright for a period long enough to enable the working out of remaining obstacles to the overall revision of the copyright law").

2

The majority makes several other arguments. First, it argues that the Clause does not require the "creation of at least one new work," *ante*, at 20, but may instead "promote the Progress of Science" in other ways. And it specifically mentions the "dissemination of existing and future works" as determinative here. *Ante,* at 20–23, and n. 25. The industry experts to whom the majority refers argue that copyright protection of already existing works can help, say, music publishers or film distributers raise prices, produce extra profits and consequently lead them to publish or distribute works they might otherwise have ignored. But ordinarily a copyright—since it is a *monopoly* on copying—*restricts* dissemination of a work once produced compared to a competitive market. And simply making the industry richer does not mean that the industry, when it makes an ordinary *forward-looking* economic calculus, will distribute works not previously distributed. The industry experts might mean that temporary extra profits will lead them to invest in the development of a market, say, by advertising. But this kind of argument, which can be made by distributers of all sorts of goods, ranging from kiwi fruit to Swedish furniture, has little if anything to do with the nonrepeatable costs of initial creation, which is the special concern of copyright protection. See *supra,* at 2–3.

Moreover, the argument proves too much. It is the kind of argument that the Stationers' Company might well have made and which the British Parliament rejected. Cf. Patterson 154–155 (describing failed booksellers' bill seeking protection from foreign competition through an extension of the copyright term). It is the kind of argument that could justify a legislature's withdrawing from the public domain the works, say, of Hawthorne or of Swift or for that matter the King James Bible in order to encourage further publication of those works; and, it could even more easily justify similar action in the case of lesser known early works, perhaps those of the Venerable Bede. The Court has not, to my knowledge, previously accepted such a rationale—a rationale well removed from the special economic circumstances that surround the nonrepeatable costs of the initial creation of a "Writing." *Supra,* at 2. And I fear that doing so would read the Copyright Clause as if it were a blank check made out in favor of those who are not themselves creators.

It is not surprising that the copyright holders' representatives who appeared before Congress did not emphasize this argument. (With one minor exception only those representatives appeared, see generally Joint Hearing; the Copyright Office did not testify, *id.*, at 239.) Rather, they focused on the Berne Convention itself. By that time, Congress had already protected all *new* works of Berne members. But it had not provided additional protection to preexisting foreign works that were then in the American public domain. Industry witnesses testified that withdrawing such works from the American public domain would permit foreign copyright owners to charge American consumers more for their products; and that, as a result, the United States would be able to persuade foreign countries to allow American holders of preexisting copyrights to charge foreign customers more money for their products. See *id.*, at 241 (statement of Eric Smith, Executive Director and General Counsel, International Intellectual Property Alliance) ("[F]ailure to [comply with

Article 18] will … undermine the ability of the United States to press other countries to implement the same sort of protection in their implementing legislation currently pending in many legislatures around the globe"); *id.*, at 253 (statement of Matt Gerson, Vice President for Congressional Affairs, Motion Picture Assn. of America) (similar). See also *id.*, at 85 (statement of Xavier Becerra, House Judiciary Committee member) ("[R]etroactivity … is probably the best way to ensure that some of our older American works, anything from Motown, to 'Star Trek,' to 'The Hardy Boys' get the protection in some of these emerging foreign markets. It is important to ensure that countries no longer use our U. S. law as an excuse for not extending retroactive copyright protections to some of our own works"). But see *id.,* at 272–279 (statement of Larry Urbanski, Chairman of the Fairness in Copyright Coalition and President of Moviecraft Inc.) (testifying against restoration on grounds similar to those set out, *supra*, at 10–13).

This argument, whatever its intrinsic merits, is an argument that directly concerns a private benefit: how to obtain more money from the sales of existing products. It is not an argument about a public benefit, such as how to promote or to protect the creative process.

Third, the majority points out that the statute "gives [authors] nothing more than the benefit of their labors during whatever time remains before the normal copyright term expires." *Ante,* at 30. But insofar as it suggests that copyright should in general help authors obtain greater monetary rewards than needed to elicit new works, it rests upon primarily European, but not American, copyright concepts. See *supra,* at 5–6.

Fourth, the majority argues that this statutory provision is necessary to fulfill our Berne Convention obligations. *Ante,* at 4–8. The Treaty, in Article 18, says that the "Convention shall apply to all works which, at the moment of its coming into force [*i.e.,* 1989 in the case of the United States] have not yet fallen into the public domain in the country of origin through the expiry of the term of protection." Berne Convention for the Protection of Literary and Artistic Works, Art. 18(1), Sept. 9, 1886, as revised at Stockholm on July 14, 1967, 828 U. N. T. S. 221, 251. The majority and Government say that this means we must protect the foreign works at issue here. And since the Berne Convention, taken as a whole, provides incentives for the creation of new works, I am willing to speculate, for argument's sake, that the statute might indirectly encourage production of new works by making the United States' place in the international copyright regime more secure.

Still, I cannot find this argument sufficient to save the statute. For one thing, this is a dilemma of the Government's own making. The United States obtained the benefits of Berne for many years despite its failure to enact a statute implementing Article 18. But in 1994, the United States and other nations signed the Agreement on Trade-Related Aspects of Intellectual Property Rights, which enabled signatories to use World Trade Organization dispute resolution mechanisms to complain about other members' Berne Convention violations. And at that time the Government, although it successfully secured reservations protecting other special features of American copyright law, made no effort to secure a reservation permitting the United States to keep some or all restored works in the American public domain. Indeed, it made no effort to do so despite the fact that Article 18 explicitly authorizes countries to negotiate exceptions to the Article's retroactivity principle. See Art. 18(3), *ibid.* ("The application of [the retroactivity] principle *shall be subject to any provisions contained in special conventions to that effect* existing or to be concluded between countries of the Union" (emphasis added)); Gervais, *Golan v. Holder*: A Look at the Constraints Imposed by the Berne Convention, 64 Vand. L. Rev. En Banc 147, 151–152 (2011); Gard, 64 Vand. L. Rev. En Banc, at 206.

For another thing, the Convention does not require Congress to enact a statute that causes so much damage to public domain material. Article 18(3) also states that "the respective countries shall determine, each in so far as it is concerned, *the conditions of application of this principle.*" 18 U. N. T. S., at 251 (emphasis added). Congress could have alleviated many of the costs that the statute imposes by, for example, creating forms of compulsory licensing, requiring "restored copyright" holders to provide necessary administrative information as a condition of protection, or insisting upon "reasonable royalties." Cf. S. 2913, 110th Cong., 2d Sess. (2008) (legislation that would have limited judicial remedies against users of orphan works); H. R. 5889, 110th Cong., 2d Sess. (2008) (House version of same); American Society of Compos- ers, Authors and Publishers, http://www.ascap.com/ licensing/termsdefined.aspx (society of music copyright owners offering blanket licenses that give users the unlimited right to perform any of its members' songs for a fixed fee, thus reducing negotiation and enforcement costs).

To say this is not to criticize the Convention or our joining it. Rather, it is to argue that the other branches of Government should have tried to *follow* the Convention and in particular its provisions offering compliance flexibility. The fact that the statute has significant First Amendment costs is relevant in this respect, for that Amendment ordinarily requires courts to evaluate less restrictive, alternative possibilities. Doing so here, reveals that neither

Congress nor the Executive took advantage of less-restrictive methods of compliance that the Convention itself provides. And that fact means that the Convention cannot provide the statute with a constitutionally sufficient justification that is otherwise lacking.

III

The fact that, by withdrawing material from the public domain, the statute inhibits an important preexisting flow of information is sufficient, when combined with the other features of the statute that I have discussed, to convince me that the Copyright Clause, interpreted in the light of the First Amendment, does not authorize Congress to enact this statute.

I respectfully dissent from the Court's contrary conclusion.

End Notes

[1] Article 18 of the Berne Convention provides:

(1) This Convention shall apply to all works which, at the moment of its coming into force, have not yet fallen into the public domain in the country of origin through the expiry of the term of protection.

(2) If, however, through the expiry of the term of protection which was previously granted, a work has fallen into the public domain of the country where protection is claimed, that work shall not be protected anew.

(3) The application of this principle shall be subject to any provisions contained in special conventions to that effect existing or to be concluded between countries of the Union. In the absence of such provisions, the respective countries shall determine, each in so far as it is concerned, the conditions of application of this principle.

(4) The preceding provisions shall also apply in the case of new accessions to the Union and to cases in which protection is extended by the application of Article 7 or by the abandonment of reservations." 828 U. N. T. S. 251.

[2] As noted by the Government's *amici*, the United States excluded foreign works from copyright not to swell the number of unprotected works available to the consuming public, but to favor domestic publishing interests that escaped paying royalties to foreign authors. See Brief for International Publishers Association et al. as *Amici Curiae* 8–15. This free-riding, according to Senator Jonathan Chace, champion of the 1891 Act, made the United States "the Barbary coast of literature" and its people "the buccaneers of books." S. Rep. No. 622, 50th Cong., 1st Sess., p. 2 (1888).

[3] See also S. Rep. No. 103–412, p. 225 (1994) ("While the United States declared its compliance with the Berne Convention in 1989, it never addressed or enacted legislation to implement Article 18 of the Convention."); Memorandum from Chris Schroeder, Counselor to the Assistant Attorney General, Office of Legal Counsel, Dept. of Justice (DOJ), to Ira S. Shapiro, General Counsel, Office of the U. S. Trade Representative (July 29, 1994), in W. Patry, Copyright and the GATT, p. C–15 (1995) ("At the time Congress was debating the BCIA, it reserved the issue of removing works from the public domain."); General

Agreement on Tariffs and Trade (GATT): Intellectual Property Provisions, Joint Hearing before the Subcommittee on Intellectual Property and Judicial Administration of the House Committee on the Judiciary and the Subcommittee on Patents, Copyrights and Trademarks of the Senate Committee on the Judiciary, 103d Cong., 2d Sess., p. 120 (1994) (URAA Joint Hearing) (app. to statement of Bruce A. Lehman, Assistant Secretary of Commerce and Commissioner of Patents and Trademarks (Commerce Dept.)) ("When the United States adhered to the Berne Convention, Congress . . . acknowledged that the possibility of restoring copyright protection for foreign works that had fallen into the public domain in the United States for failure to comply with formalities was an issue that merited further discussion.").

[4] The dissent implicitly agrees that, whatever tentative conclusion Congress reached in 1988, Article 18 requires the United States to "protect the foreign works at issue," at least absent a special conven- tion the United States did not here negotiate. *Post*, at 22. See also *post,* at 23 (citing Gervais, *Golan* v. *Holder*: A Look at the Constraints Imposed by the Berne Convention, 64 Vand. L. Rev. En Banc 147, 151–152 (2011)); *id.,* at 152 ("[T]he Convention clearly requires that *some* level of protection be given to foreign authors whose works have entered the public domain (other than by expiration of previous copyright)."). Accord S. Ricketson, The Berne Convention for the Protection of Literary and Artistic Works 1886–1986, p. 675 (1987)
("There is no basis on which [protection of existing works under Article 18] can be completely denied. The conditions and reservations," authorized by Article 18(3) [and stressed by the dissent, *post*, at 23–24] are of "limited" and "transitional" duration and "would not be permitted to deny [protection] altogether in relation to a particular class . . . of works.").

[5] NAFTA ultimately included a limited retroactivity provision—a precursor to §514 of the URAA—granting U. S. copyright protection to certain Mexican and Canadian films. These films had fallen into the public domain, between 1978 and 1988, for failure to meet U. S. notice requirements. See North American Free Trade Agreement Implementation Act, §334, 107 Stat. 2115; Brief for Franklin Pierce Center for Intellectual Property as *Amicus Curiae* 14–16. One year later, Congress replaced this provision with the version of 17 U. S. C. §104A at issue here. See 3 M. Nimmer & D. Nimmer, Copyright §9A.03, 9A.04, pp. 9A–17, 9A–22 (2011) (hereinafter Nimmer).

[6] This tension between the United States and its new Berne counter parties calls into question the dissent's assertion that, despite the 1988 Act's minimalist approach, "[t]he United States obtained the benefits of Berne for many years." *Post*, at 22–23. During this six-year period, Congress had reason to doubt that U. S. authors enjoyed the *full* benefits of Berne membership.

[7] Marrakesh Agreement Establishing the World Trade Organization, Apr. 15, 1994, 1867 U. N. T. S. 154.

[8] Proponents of prompt congressional action urged that avoiding a trade enforcement proceeding—potentially the WTO's first—would be instrumental in preserving the United States' "reputation as a world leader in the copyright field." URAA Joint Hearing 241 (statement of Eric Smith, International Intellectual Property Alliance (IIPA)). In this regard, U. S. negotiators reported that widespread perception of U. S. noncompliance was undermining our leverage in copyright negotiations. Unimpeachable adherence to Berne, Congress was told, would help ensure enhanced foreign protection, and hence profitable dissemination, for existing and future U. S. works. See *id.,* at 120 (app. to statement of Lehman, Commerce Dept.) ("Clearly providing for [retroactive] protection for existing

works in our own law will improve our position in future negotiations."); *id.*, at 268 (statement of Berman, RIAA).

[9] Title 17 U. S. C. §104A is reproduced in full in an appendix to this opinion.

[10] Works from most, but not all, foreign countries are eligible for protection under §514. The provision covers only works that have "at least one author or rightholder who was, at the time the work was created, a national or domiciliary of an eligible country." 17 U. S. C. §104A(h)(6)(D). An "eligible country" includes any "nation, other than the United States, that—(A) becomes a WTO member country after the date of the enactment of the [URAA]; [or] (B) on such date of enactment is, or after such date of enactment becomes, a nation adhering to the Berne Convention." §104A(h)(3). As noted above, see *supra*, at 3, 164 countries adhere to the Berne Convention. World Intellectual Property Organization, Contracting Parties: Berne Convention, www.wipo.int/treaties (as visited Jan. 13, 2012, and in Clerk of Court's case file).

[11] From the first Copyright Act until late in the 20th century, Congress conditioned copyright protection on compliance with certain statutory formalities. The most notable required an author to register her work, renew that registration, and affix to published copies notice of copyrighted status. The formalities drew criticism as a trap for the unwary. See, *e.g.*, 2 Nimmer §7.01[A], p. 7–8; Doyle, Cary, McCannon, & Ringer, Notice of Copyright, Study No. 7, p. 46 (1957), reprinted in 1 Studies on Copyright 229, 272 (1963).

In 1976, Congress eliminated the registration renewal requirement for future works. Copyright Act of 1976, §302, 408, 90 Stat. 2572, 2580. In 1988, it repealed the mandatory notice prerequisite. BCIA §7, 102 Stat. 2857. And in 1992, Congress made renewal automatic for works still in their first term of protection. Copyright Amendments Act of 1992, 106 Stat. 264–266. The Copyright Act retains, however, incentives for authors to register their works and provide notice of the works' copyrighted status. See, *e.g.*, 17 U. S. C. §405(b) (precluding actual and statutory damages against "innocent infringers" of a work that lacked notice of copyrighted status); §411(a) (requiring registration of U. S. "work[s]," but not foreign works, before an owner may sue for infringement). The revisions successively made accord with Berne Convention Article 5(2), which proscribes application of copyright formalities to foreign authors. Berne, however, affords domestic authors no escape from domestic formalities. See Art. 5(3) (protection within country of origin is a matter of domestic law).

[12] Title 17 U. S. C. §104A(h)(6)(B) defines a "restored work" to exclude "an original work of authorship" that is "in the public domain in its source country through expiration of [its] term of protection." This provision tracks Berne's denial of protection for any work that has "fallen into the public domain in the country of origin through the expiry of the term of protection." Art. 18(1), 828 U. N. T. S., at 251.

[13] Restoration is a misnomer insofar as it implies that all works protected under §104A previously enjoyed protection. Each work in the public domain because of lack of national eligibility or subject-matter protection, and many that failed to comply with formalities, never enjoyed U. S. copyright protection. See, *e.g.*, 3 Nimmer §9A.04[A][1][b][iii], at 9A–26, and n. 29.4.

[14] A reliance party must have used the work in a manner that would constitute infringement had a valid copyright been in effect. See §104A(h)(4)(A). After restoration, the reliance party is limited to her previous uses. A performer of a restored work, for example, cannot, post-restoration, venture to sell copies of the script. See 3 Nimmer §9A.04[C][1][a], at 9A–45 to 9A–46.

[15] Petitioners' complaint also challenged the constitutionality of the Copyright Term Extension Act, 112 Stat. 2827, which added 20 years to the duration of existing and future copyrights.

After this Court rejected a similar challenge in *Eldred* v. *Ashcroft*, 537 U. S. 186 (2003), the District Court dismissed this portion of petitioners' suit on the pleadings, *Golan* v. *Ashcroft*, 310 F. Supp. 2d 1215 (D. Colo. 2004). The Tenth Circuit affirmed, *Golan* v. *Gonzales*, 501 F. 3d 1179 (2007), and petitioners do not attempt to revive that claim in this Court, Pet. for Cert. 7, n. 2. Neither have petitioners challenged the District Court's entry of summary judgment for the Government on the claim that §514 violates the substantive component of the Due Process Clause.

[16] Cf. 3 Nimmer §9A.02[A][2], at 9A–11, n. 28 ("[I]t stretches the language of the Berne Convention past the breaking point to posit that following 'expiry of the zero term' the . . . work need not be resurrected.").

[17] See B. Bugbee, Genesis of American Patent and Copyright Law 123–124 (1967) (hereinafter Bugbee) (Delaware, Maryland, and Pennsylvania).

[18] See 1783 Mass. Acts p. 236; 1783 N. J. Laws p. 47; 1783 N. H. Laws p. 521; 1783 R. I. Laws pp. 6–7; 1784 S. C. Acts p. 49; 1785 Va. Acts ch. VI; 1786 N. Y. Laws p. 298.

[19] 1783 Conn. Pub. Acts no. 617; 1783 N. J. Laws p. 47; 1785 N. C. Laws p. 563; 1786 Ga. Laws p. 323. In four States, copyright enforcement was restricted to works "not yet printed" or "hereinafter published." 1783 Mass. Acts p. 236; 1783 N. H. Laws p. 521; 1783 R. I. Laws pp. 6–7; 1784 S. C. Acts p. 49.

[20] See Bugbee 109–123.

[21] The parties debate the extent to which the First Congress removed works from the public domain. We have held, however, that at least some works protected by the 1790 Act previously lacked protection. In *Wheaton* v. *Peters*, 8 Pet. 591 (1834), the Court ruled that before enactment of the 1790 Act, common-law copyright protection expired upon first publication. *Id.*, at 657, 663. Thus published works covered by the 1790 Act previously would have been in the public domain unless protected by state statute. Had the founding generation perceived the constitutional boundary petitioners advance today, the First Congress could have designed a prospective scheme that left the public domain undisturbed. Accord *Luck's Music Library, Inc.* v. *Gonzales*, 407 F. 3d 1262, 1265 (CADC 2005) (Section 514 does not offend the Copyright Clause because, *inter alia*, "evidence from the First Congress," as confirmed by *Wheaton*, "points toward constitutionality.").

[22] Here, as in *Eldred*, "[b]ecause the Clause empowering Congress to confer copyrights also authorizes patents, congressional practice with respect to patents informs our inquiry." 537 U. S., at 201.

[23] Section 514 is in line with these measures; like them, it accords protection to works that had lapsed into the public domain because of failure to comply with U. S. statutory formalities. See *supra*, at 9, and n. 11.

[24] Legislation of this order, petitioners argue, is best understood as an exercise of Congress' power to remedy excusable neglect. Even so, the remedy sheltered creations that, absent congressional action, would have been open to free exploitation. Such action, according to petitioners' dominant argument, see *supra*, at 13–14, is ever and always impermissible. Accord *Luck's Music Library*, 407 F. 3d, at 1265–1266 ("Plaintiffs urge that [the 1790 Act and the wartime legislation] simply extended the time limits for filing and [did] not purport to modify the prohibition on removing works from the public domain. But to the extent that potential copyright holders failed to satisfy procedural requirements, such works"—like those protected by §514—"would necessarily have already entered the public domain . . . .").

[25] But see Brief for Motion Picture Association of America as *Amicus Curiae* 27 (observing that income from existing works can finance the creation and publication of new works); *Eldred*,

537 U. S., at 208, n. 15 (noting that Noah Webster "supported his entire family from the earnings on his speller and grammar during the twenty years he took to complete his dictionary" (internal quotation marks omitted)).

[26] The dissent also suggests, more tentatively, that at least where copyright legislation extends protection to works previously in the public domain, Congress must counterbalance that restriction with new incentives to create. *Post*, at 8. Even assuming the public domain were a category of constitutional significance, contra *supra,* at 13–19, we would not understand "the Progress of Science" to have this contingent meaning.

[27] That the same economic incentives might also induce the dissemination of futons, fruit, or Bibles, see *post*, at 20, is no answer to this evidence that legislation furthering the dissemination of literary property has long been thought a legitimate way to "promote the Progress of Science."

[28] The dissent suggests that the "utilitarian view of copyrigh[t]" embraced by Jefferson, Madison, and our case law sets us apart from continental Europe and inhibits us from harmonizing our copyright laws with those of countries in the civil-law tradition. See *post*, at 5–6, 22. For persuasive refutation of that suggestion, see Austin, Does the Copyright Clause Mandate Isolationism? 26 Colum. J. L. & Arts 17, 59 (2002) (cautioning against "an isolationist reading of the Copyright Clause that is in tension with . . . America's international copyright relations over the last hundred or so years").

[29] On the initial appeal in this case, the Tenth Circuit gave an unconfined reading to our reference in *Eldred* to "traditional contours of copyright." 501 F. 3d, at 1187–1196. That reading was incorrect, as we here clarify.

[30] See *Eldred,* 537 U. S., at 221 ("Protection of [an author's original expression from unrestricted exploitation] does not raise the free speech concerns present when the government compels or burdens the communication of particular facts or ideas.").

[31] Focusing narrowly on the specific problem of orphan works, the dissent overlooks these principal protections against "the dissemination-restricting harms of copyright." *Post*, at 14.

[32] "[R]equir[ing] works that have already fallen into the public domain to stay there" might, as the dissent asserts, supply an "easily administrable standard." *Post*, at 14. However attractive this bright-line rule might be, it is not a rule rooted in the constitutional text or history. Nor can it fairly be gleaned from our case law. The dissent cites three decisions to document its assertion that "this Court has assumed the particular importance of public domain material in roughly analogous circumstances." *Post*, at 15. The dictum in *Graham* v. *John Deere Co. of Kansas City,* 383 U. S. 1, 6 (1966), noted earlier, did not treat the public domain as a constitutional limit—certainly not under the rubric of the First Amendment. See *supra,* at 19. The other two decisions the dissent cites considered whether the federal Patent Act preempted a state trade-secret law, *Kewanee Oil Co.* v. *Bicron Corp.*, 416 U. S. 470, 479–484 (1974), and whether the freedom of the press shielded reporters from liability for publishing material drawn from public court documents, *Cox Broadcasting Corp.* v. *Cohn*, 420 U. S. 469, 495–497 (1975). Neither decision remotely ascribed constitutional significance to a work's public domain status.

[33] It was the Fifth Amendment's Takings Clause—not the First Amendment—that Congress apparently perceived to be a potential check on its authority to protect works then freely available to the public. See URAA Joint Hearing 3 (statement of Rep. Hughes); *id.,* at 121 (app. to statement of Lehman, Commerce Dept.); *id.,* at 141 (statement of Shapiro, USTR); *id.,* at 145 (statement of Christopher Schroeder, DOJ). The reliance-party protections supplied by §514, see *supra,* at 10–11, were meant to address such concerns. See URAA Joint Hearing 148–149 (prepared statement of Schroeder).

[34] Because Shostakovich was a pre-1973 Russian composer, his works were not protected in the United States. See U. S. Copyright Office, Circular No. 38A: The International Copyright Relations of the United States 9, 11, n. 2 (2010) (copyright relations between the Soviet Union and the United States date to 1973).

[35] Persistently deploring "'restored copyright' protection [because it] removes material from the public domain," *post*, at 14, the dissent does not pause to consider when and why the material came to be lodged in that domain. Most of the works affected by §514 got there after a term of zero or a term cut short by failure to observe U. S. formalities. See *supra,* at 9.

[36] The pervasive problem of copyright piracy, noted *post*, at 13, likewise is scarcely limited to protected foreign works formerly in the public domain.

INDEX

A

abuse, 46
access, 16, 19, 20, 28, 33, 34
accessions, 21, 60
accommodations, 16, 18, 20, 31
alters, 9, 10, 11
assets, 41
authorities, 22
authority, 2, 11, 16, 17, 18, 20, 24, 25, 28, 29, 30, 40, 64

B

barriers, 16, 20
beneficiaries, 53
benefits, 44, 47, 58, 61
bounds, 26
breeding, 52
businesses, 2, 7

C

calculus, 56
case law, 44, 46, 64
censorship, 24
challenges, 7
classroom, 31
commercial, 22, 51
communication, 31, 64
community, 28, 46
compatibility, 23
compensation, 24, 38, 46, 52
competition, 44, 57
compliance, vii, 1, 2, 6, 11, 18, 21, 23, 25, 27, 30, 36, 59, 60, 62
composers, 8
computer, 44
confinement, 17, 25
congress, 28
consent, 4
constitutional limitations, 20
construction, 17, 26, 27
consumers, 50, 57
contour, 11, 31
convention, 27
conviction, 43
cost, 8, 34, 51
counterbalance, 63
country of origin, viii, 5, 16, 20, 21, 23, 58, 60, 62
covering, 27
creative process, 18, 30, 58
creativity, 11
criticism, 4, 31, 62
customers, 57

D

damages, iv, 4, 62
database, 51
denial, 62
deprivation, 34
dichotomy, 18, 31, 34
diffusion, 30
disposition, 41, 45
dissenting opinion, 19, 53
distribution, 4, 51
drawing, 53

E

earnings, 63
earthquakes, 55
economic incentives, 64
education, 50
educators, vii, 2, 8
eligibility criteria, 48
eligible countries, 42
encouragement, 43, 46
enforcement, viii, 16, 22, 23, 24, 32, 59, 61, 63
enlargement, 18, 31
evidence, 18, 63, 64
exercise, 3, 4, 5, 11, 63
exploitation, 10, 19, 28, 31, 34, 38, 63, 64

F

fair use, 4, 18, 19, 31, 32, 34
false belief, 52
fear, 57
films, 43, 51, 61
flexibility, 30, 59
flour, 27, 55
force, 5, 39, 41, 58, 60
foreign affairs, 25
formation, 27
framing, 30
freedom, 7, 18, 31, 52, 53, 64
fruits, 46

G

grants, 3, 16, 20, 43, 44, 49, 54

H

history, 18, 28, 44, 48, 64
host, 35
hurricanes, 55

I

income, 63
individuals, 7
industries, 18, 30
industry, 56
intellectual property, 1, 6, 18, 29
interference, 33
inventions, 17, 28
inventors, 43, 46, 47, 55
investment, 18, 30

J

justification, 55, 59

L

landscape, 22
laws, 20, 46, 53, 56
lead, 56
learning, 11, 17, 29, 30, 43, 45
legal protection, 3
legislation, 10, 11, 17, 27, 28, 29, 35, 47, 53, 56, 57, 59, 60, 63, 64
lens, 44
lifetime, 21
light, 16, 24, 26, 53, 60
litigation, 27

M

machinery, 27
majority, 7, 42, 53, 54, 55, 56, 58
manufacturing, 42
marketing, 54
marketplace, 34, 50
materials, 7, 24, 28, 35, 51
matter, 23, 35, 42, 53, 54, 55, 57, 62
media, 54
membership, 12, 61
monopoly, 4, 44, 45, 46, 47, 56
motivation, 47
museums, 51
music, 3, 34, 47, 50, 51, 54, 56, 59
musicians, 16, 20

N

neglect, 63
negotiating, 50
negotiation, 51, 59
neutral, 3, 9

O

obstacles, 56
ownership, 3, 33, 39

P

pain, viii, 16, 22
patents, 6, 17, 28, 45, 46, 47, 53, 55, 63
pedigree, 32
performers, vii, 2, 8
permission, 1, 3, 4, 5, 44, 50, 51
permit, 17, 27, 32, 39, 57
photographs, 33, 44, 51
piracy, 18, 30, 52, 65
policy, 35, 47, 53
precedent, 48
precedents, 25
private benefits, 44
profit, 4
property rights, 52
publishing, 53, 60, 64

R

reading, 11, 17, 27, 48, 64
recognition, 46
regulations, 39
relief, 4, 40
remediation, 25
rent, 54
reporters, 64
reproduction, 4, 31
reputation, 61
requirements, 23, 37, 42, 48, 52, 61, 63
resistance, 35
resolution, 6, 22, 35, 53, 59
resources, 12
response, 16, 20, 23, 29, 35
restoration, 2, 18, 23, 28, 30, 32, 36, 37, 38, 39, 40, 41, 48, 50, 51, 58, 62
restrictions, 11, 13, 48, 52
retaliation, 23
rewards, 43, 58
rights, viii, 2, 3, 4, 5, 10, 13, 16, 18, 21, 23, 28, 31, 32, 33, 34, 42, 45, 46, 47
rings, 48
risk, 53
royalty, 4, 34, 52

S

sanctions, 6, 22
scholarship, 4, 31
school, 50
science, 18, 29, 30, 47
scope, 30, 55
society, 51, 59
specter, 23
speech, 2, 3, 7, 9, 10, 11, 13, 18, 24, 32, 33, 34, 53, 54, 64
statutes, 27, 34, 45, 46, 54, 55
stress, 33

suppression, 9, 11, 45

T

teachers, 2
teeth, 23
telephone, 39, 40
tension, 61, 64
territory, 20
threats, 23
tracks, 62
trade, 6, 20, 22, 44, 53, 61, 64
trademarks, 6
trading partners, 3, 9, 23
traditions, 10
translation, 38, 40
treaties, 12, 62
treatment, 25, 26, 36, 54

U

uniform, 27
universities, 51

V

vote, 7, 10

W

war, 28
withdrawal, 56
witnesses, 57